The Legal Mafia

How Child Protective Services Kidnap & Sell Children

By
Mina Ghiate

Everything is real in this book

DEDICATION

To every child and family
has been
victimized by the corrupt
system.

CHAPTERS

INTRODUCTION

Here I am, once again, back to the scene of darkness. Here I am, exhausted from living under all the forms of oppression. My children and I still suffer from miscarriages of justice and deprivation.

We are treated unfairly and brutally. We are subjected to torture and humiliation, and we are prevented from obtaining our rights. As a result of this dehumanization process, we are counted among the forgotten, marginalized and despised. Whenever we demand justice, we get struck by damage owing to gross negligence and undisguised contempt on the part of the Italian authority. Our voices are NEVER heard!

This is how I am with my painful tragedy. It is a tragedy whose events are written with a spate of pain, torment, and a sense of inferiority. It is the story of a woman who carried her dreams and aspirations to another country in search of a better life. Only to find out that I went to an absolute hell that changed my life and the lives of my children.

My two beloved little girls were questionably, forcibly taken away from me by Child Protective Service and Juvenile Court. They used deceit and deception for the sole objective of kidnapping and trafficking for profit.

In the case of social workers, their power is absolute and is given to them to abduct children and accuse parents unjustly. They can enter your home without any warrant, and forcefully remove your children without giving cause or reason. The vast majority of cases where families have lost their children have done absolutely nothing wrong.

To justify their abduction, social workers would accuse you of abusing your children, and you would be jailed unlawfully. Every year, many good parents feel they are guilty until proven innocent.

Most people feel secure in the belief that the system is there to protect them from "the wicked." This belief is unrealistic and dangerous. It is an insidious monster that can and does prey upon the innocent, the vulnerable and the ordinary law-abiding citizens of Italian country.

Would you ever expect a gang of crooks to care about their victims? Do you think a criminal authority would ever look after you? Do you trust the mafia to keep you safe? If you answered no to these questions, then why would you ever expect the government to care about you? You are not the government's customer, you are not a citizen they represent, nor are you a person they care to help. You are their victim, and they wish to exploit you, to devalue you, and to deprive you of what you hold dear.

Injustice, corruption, cruelty and crimes happen in many courtrooms and in plain sight. The world of juvenile courts, judges, social workers, and their employees - is appalling beyond imagining. It is a world with plenty of events exceeding horror stories. The events remarkably reflect a sick system that decides the fate of entire families and the future of many children.

By taking advantage of their position of power, they are able to easily maintain the illusion that they represent children's best interest, when we can empirically discern that they represent themselves instead. The more funds they receive, the more their crimes against our families are committed.

The minor has become an easy bite between the fangs of human wolves who connive to facilitate the trade of thousands of children. They viciously mistreat the most innocent. This legal mafia, funded by the people of this nation, runs a BIG BUSINESS that is worth five billion euros each year.

If the government gives more rewards just because the more children are removed from their families, then the state serves no meaningful purpose except to satiate the desires of the individuals who reap the benefits of destroying families.

The funding continues as long as the child is out of the home. When a child in foster care is placed with a new family or in an institution, then bonus funds are available. The judicial part gets more funding by handling more cases. There is no money to be made by doing the right, the ethical, and the moral. Family-Juvenile Judges do not admit errant action. They do not preserve the right of the child and the parent, or seek to do the right for family reunification.

This book will discuss evidence derived from real sources about how a government lucrative market exists, and how Italian and foreign children are being snatched and sold to sex shops, homosexuals, and people with severe mental health issues. These people, in turn, abuse the children emotionally, physically, and sexually

As the author of the book, I have stood out as someone who has taken control and has directed her energy into a fight for justice. And as I write from the deepest part of my heart, I want the voices of angels who still cry for liberty and love to be heard. The terrified poor children who have become orphans overnight even though their parents are alive. They are ignored, abused, and exploited without their perception or desire, but with pain and grief.

I will reveal in vivid detail how the heinous and inhuman acts of child trafficking are being committed so that they can be brought to light. This book is a rage against family abuse and child abuse. It is about the struggle I take up, about the heartbreaking illegal adoption system and the unjust Italian judiciary.

For your own safety and the safety of your loved ones, you need to know how the system works, its capabilities and motivations, and how to protect yourself from falling victim to it.

The long-hidden business of minors and the stolen child-hood will shock and anger anyone who wants to face the truth about the dark and sordid Italian legal kidnapping.

CHAPTER ONE

MY CHILDREN SHOCKING ABDUCTION

After I had broken up with my first husband, the father of my children, I travelled to Italy and I got remarried an Italian citizen in the province of Reggio Emilia, Northern Italy. I took my daughters with me in 2006 when they were 8 and 5 years old. Life was happy and calm in the beginning, but soon the Italian husband turned it into a real nightmare. He became violent and hit my two little girls. As I was afraid for their safety, I turned to the local social services for guidance and help.

I never imagined that social workers could be the most despicable people. They pretend to protect children while they abuse them. After my little girls and I had taken to the emergency room for medical visits, doctors found slight bruises in my children. And since they are very precise, they even examined my children's intimate parts.

So, the medical records confirmed that "the genital parts of both girls are intact," and they had never been subjected to sexual violence; no one wanted to take that into consideration which would unfairly lead to an endless nightmare that I am going to explain.

Anyway, after the medical examinations had been completed, my daughters and I were placed in a social residential care for a few days. Suddenly, the social workers and the policemen showed up and removed my daughters; my older was placed in foster family, and my younger was placed in foster institute called "Cenacolo Francescano," in Reggio Emilia city. Bearing in mind this displacement was followed by illegal adoption. It seemed to be all what social workers wanted: It is a "legal kidnapping."

We have experienced harsh behaviours from social workers, educators, judges, therapists, and others such as those who "pick up" children. We have been driven to destruction. Words cannot describe our devastating experience!

I naively imagined that social workers would help me. I did not know the truth about them and about Juvenile Judges who carry out corrupt business on the skin of children. Years of torment, trivial, and disguised decrees issued by juvenile court were aimed only to pass the time.

My children were snatched from everyone and everything dear to them. They suffered horrific physical and psychological abuse by Child Protective Services. And they were kidnapped and sold by the juvenile court of Bologna city. They're now adults but they haven't return to me yet.

I resorted to local social services for temporary help. But instead of getting assistance and support, I was severely deprived of my beloved little girls, and falsely accused of abusing them.

Barbaric manner to snatch my children

The kidnapping of my daughters is still etched in my memory since that dreary day. Every day that passes me I feel as though my daughters are being snatched from me every moment, and my heart is burning with every snatch.

They dragged my little girls as if they had led someone condemned to death. Policemen and social workers pounced on my daughters, just like a wolf when it pounces on its prey. They brutally took my little girls out of me while were holding me with all their might. They were terrified, cried, screamed for help, and begged with heartburn and pain: "Don't leave us Mum, they will kill us''

Their cries were tearing my heart, I was trying my best to take them back to me, but social workers were constantly pushing me back, and one of the policemen twisted my arm with such force that it almost broke. A surge of horror flowed into me; I was about to succumb to death.

Three of policemen and two social workers drove my little girls into the car unwillingly. They were permanently traumatised and suffered from double-shock; the horror of the violent and inhumane behaviour on the one hand, and the sudden separation from me on the other hand.

I was also left severely traumatised that I can't recover. I felt that I was dragged by stream into a dark ocean while the darkness was suffocating me, I cried out of sadness: "Leave me and my daughters in peace," but my cries were unheard. I was left hopeless, fearful, alone suffering waves of infinite loss.

Monsters snapped my children without pity or mercy. They have ripped my soul out, and I have no longer wished to live. I feel like I am in prison. Our souls are executed, and our happiness is spoiled. How can one be so cruel to weak people? What is behind urgent measures if they do not help anyone?

The story of the forced and unjustified removal of my children makes me deeply regret trusting the disguised social workers. I was deceived when I thought they were serving the citizens. In fact, they are cruel and dead inside. They kill innocent people and dance over their corpses!

The social protective services, in Italy, are no longer for child protection. They are only trying to hide behind that. It is sheer hypocrisy. I didn't imagine that social work could be degraded and valueless. I was naive like many other parents who have been trapped because of their naivety and trust. They are voluntarily driven to restrictions and controls that kill children's souls and curb the parents' feelings.

So, they became to cling to blind justice that leads to destruction. Only to remain battered and bruised by the tyranny of these local government-funded courts as the judges, social workers, and their psychologists mock the outraged parents. When I requested a temporary help from social workers, they pretended to assist. I later learnt that they betrayed me to kidnap my children. How come a citizen who seeks help suddenly finds themselves without children?!

I requested support in a time of difficulty as I wanted to break up with my violent husband for my daughters' safety. Unexpectedly, I found myself forced, for no real reason, to part with my children who are paying for this abuse. This sense of injustice that is expressed by my daughters and me demonstrates the illegality of the situation.

The trauma that is derived from the separation between the mother and the children, of which my daughters have given ample evidence, is a behaviour that is criminal, to say the least.

My children were forced to live in inadequate foster care and adoption with strangers. And when I requested to transfer them to my new home, my voice remained unheard. Moreover, and I was unjustly prevented from any contact with them. I have jumped through every hoop known to man to get my daughters back. But I have always been denied, and my request has always been neglected.

The prevalence of social worker discretion allows removal of children based on claims of "endangering the welfare of a child" without providing specifics or devising a safety plan to keep a child with a good parent. They all lie, it's happening to everyone, and it's happening nationwide. Social protective services don't work for children's well-being; they overwhelmingly deprive them from good parents.

The removal of my children was unnecessary because I didn't abuse them, and I didn't abandon them. So, why they were removed from me? What was the real cause behind it?

Actually, there is no real reason on my part, but there is a conflict of interest based on fraud, deception and perjury from child social 'abduction' services and Juvenile Judges.

I took my daughters from my country to grow up in front of my eyes. They are not only part of me, but also are my soul, and my life. Taking them away from me was not the ideal option. Much harm has been done to my children in foster care, and the strong ties between me and them was completely destroyed. The message that was sent to my children was that I had abandoned them. Contrary to that, I still mourn their loss that literally causes lifelong pain and trauma to me.

The corrupt system punished my children when they were in desperate need of help. The social workers were dishonest with me and misrepresented the evidence. I used to go to juvenile court to copy and read reports that social workers and psychologists wrote. I found out that the evidence was always distorted and against which I had no recourse. The fact that they are immune from prosecution even if they present evidence that it is all lies and slander.

I felt that I had no hope and fell into despair. I had problems where a competent and compassionate social worker could have intervened to rectify the situation. But instead of offering assistance to us, my two daughters were treated horribly and deprived of me.

When they came to this world, I loved them, and I made it my mission to shower them with love every day since their birth. I had an idea that they were mine and that I was theirs, and we would remain together forever. I could not imagine that someday they would not remain my daughters. Only those beautiful memories remain, passing in front of my eyes like a movie, tearing my heart apart once, and planting hope within me once again. The world became gloomy without them. Deep sea of sorrows that words cannot describe!

Every day I wonder: Where are my precious, beloved girls? Where are my fragrant roses in which all the colours meet? Where are their innocent laughs that were sounding throughout the place? Where are their wonderful, innocent drawings that I used to hang on the wall and made them feel that I was proud of what they did. Waves of nostalgia pierce my heart!

I miss their words: "Mum we love you. Mum we are happy to be with you." I miss their talking to me of everything that was on their mind. I miss accompanying them to buy gifts and to play together in their best-loved park as we used to. I miss calling them by their names to eat their favourite meals as I used to. I miss telling stories to them before they sleep as happily as I used to.

My house is dark without them, and my life is dark without them. I wake each day to thoughts of them. Their voices echo in my head all day long. How can I survive without my children? Wounds, fantasies, scars, groans, and different scenes of heartbreak that words cannot heal!

The harm that was brought to my children and me has aroused a deep sense of injustice inside us. It killed my daughters' souls and dignity. They used to fly with joy and tender gentle smiles in my presence. They didn't know that someone could surprise them with situations that would stab at their hearts.

We, the parents, cannot get past the fact that these cursed institutions steal our beloved children and sell them for money. It is crushing explosions in our homes that burn our families and our children. It is chaos and betrayal in Italian government institutions. The explosions of its cold war reverberate in our homes and ruin their peace and stability. Our children become victims of this war; dead but alive. These criminal government institutions pursue and destroy innocent people every day and anywhere in Italy.

Day after day passes, and these institutions continue to do what looks like camouflage for families; they drown them in fabricated dreams to the point of fatigue and suddenly throw them into a war of nerves and exhaustion of feelings.

There are only fake promises and decrees which have been turned into tools for mass killing that makes the minds suffocated; the more the resistance of victims increases, the more these criminals release false reports and slanderous accusations. And under the slogan of protection and security, they kill parents and children with delusive drawings and deadly psychotherapy sessions.

This war should not be overlooked by parents for a moment. It is important than anything else to protect children from this current infernal system where our hopes and our existence are burnt. All families need to be alert to the fact that there are social workers who are dishonest to the extent that they are willing to put people at risk.

The minor has the right to live in his own family

The purpose of the alternative care institution is not, however, to provide 'children' to couples without their own children or to singles, nor to give a 'guaranteed' salary to those who want to profit by taking advantage of the misfortunes of others, but to provide support to the family of origin that momentarily and for various reasons in a state of need.

Supporting families and not taking advantage of their difficult situation and deprive them of her children. Total removal of a child from their family should only be done in extreme cases. Success in protecting children should never be measured in the number of adoptions completed, but in the number of adoptions that have been prevented by saving their families.

In this regard, the law is clear: every minor has the right to live in his own family. This right sanctioned by art. 30 and 31 of the Italian Constitution which respectively establish the right and duty of parents to maintain, educate, educate their children and the obligation of the Republic to facilitate the formation of the family and the fulfillment of related tasks with economic measures and other provisions, and regulated by **law 184/1983 ('Law 184'** entitled 'right of the child to a family', modified by **Law no. 149/01** with the introduction of important changes)

Title I, 'Right of the child to his own family'. Art, 1 states that:

1. The minor has the right to grow and be educated within his own family.
2. The condition of indigence of the parents or of the parent exercising parental authority cannot be an obstacle to the enforcement of the right of the minor to his or her family. To this end, support and help interventions are arranged in favour of the family.
3. The state, the regions, and the local end, within the scope of their own competencies, support, with suitable interventions, respecting their autonomy and within the limits of the available financial resources, families at risk, in order to prevent abandonment and to allow the minor to be educated within his own family.

That's all. This is the aim, the 'ratio' of a law that could not be clearer than this, just as, in this regard, the Italian Constitution is equally clear. The purpose of alternative care in this perspective also recognised at an international level, of safeguarding the family of origin, the custody of the minor can only be temporary.

The temporariness is a temporary moment of difficulty for the family of origin that can be compensated for with the intervention of the foster family. Custody is temporary by definition, precisely because its purpose is the return of the child to the family of origin once the difficulties are over.

The placement of a child in foster care should be viewed with extreme seriousness, and only in the interest of the well-being of the child. It should only occur if absolutely necessary. Ending parental rights is a devastating and tragic outcome. Fostering adoption should be the absolute last resort. The government should not be in the business of creating orphans.

In its place, there needs to be a system that is truly in the best interests of the children. And if at all possible, children belong with their family. Child social service needs oversight, accountability, and consequences. And unless conditions are safe, children should be returned to their families. But the system is not truly “in the best interest of the children”.

If we go back in time, as early as 2011/2012, conferences entitled "forced abduction of minors from families" was held in various cities of Italy. The data that came out of the conference halls were and still are worrying: "80% of cases of removal of children are made for false accusations."

These criminals are beyond incredible, they are tougher than wild animals; instead of protecting children and assisting families, they are devastating them! They are always fighting parents; destroying parents becomes the focus of their job. Sending parents to jail is a powerful deterrent to continue their abuses freely.

CHAPTER TWO

SOCIAL WORKERS KIDNAP AND JUDGES APPROVE

Bureaucratic betrayal of "parental incapacity"

When an unfair judge wears the robe of justice–a great disaster generates. You will not find a law to protect you. You will be definitely humiliated. You will seem dead in life and will suffer grief. The ignominy of total defeat will make you feel ashamed, silly, and stupid. It's something beyond indignity! Then you will reach out to ask for help from an official to capture your stolen humanity but in vain. This is how I am with my tragedy.

In the juvenile court of Bologna city, you cannot expect an evaluation or analysis of a case from a judge, but you can see a decree that is issued very easily; a decision which not depend on effective documentation or evidence. Social workers propose removing the children, and the juvenile court recognizes the child removal immediately and without verifying the case.

It is a serious violation that leads to illegal foster care and adoption. Just as it happened in my case dealt with by Judge Francesca Salvatore. She employed the concept of 'parental incompetence' as a catch phrase to justify her kidnapping of my two daughters, this incompetence which was absolutely not proved. It is clear that it is this judge who must undergo a procedure to determine her competence. Because of her irresponsibility and wickedness my children were taken from me and placed in foster care and adoption.

Although my children were clinging to me and did not want to leave me, the juvenile judge and social workers trampled on their wishes instead of appreciating the mother-child solid bond and the true affection, they considered me as an inappropriate and unable to take care of my children.

But the core of the question here: Was the alleged competence really checked? Who can identify parental eligibility? And who can define what is best for children and their well-being?

According to the law, before removing a child, parental ability must be assessed to determine or measure the competence of one or both parents. In order to perform this task, the parent's capability must be determined by experts and specialists through a careful evaluation of the parents' personality; otherwise, this is theft and abuse.

Furthermore, “parental incompetence” is actually pure treason: a bureaucratic betrayal under the guise of a good mother or a good father, which hides a conflict of interest. Ripped children pay a lot to the professionals who invade them. Most of these professionals are not always up to the task and above all are not always on children’s side. They conspire with others who have already broken the great pact that institutions should sign with this wounded childhood.

The phantom “parental incompetence”: the name that justifies the actions by which children are separated from their parents, tracing this competence/inability to a psychological characteristic, that is to say, to a personality trait, is also a scientific abuse.

There is no category or syndrome of parental incompetence in any textbook of psychology or psychiatry. There is no parental incompetence as a psychological category subject to exclusion. The acts so frequently used by the Courts for Minors in Italy, of entrusting a minor to third parties (Social Services) is a hypothesis that should be prosecuted only for very serious and exceptional reasons.

The child has the right to live with his natural parents and to maintain a balanced and continuous relationship with them, and even with his grandparents and relatives. The child has the right to express his opinion and feelings in every procedure or decision that may affect him/her.

However, the child's voice remains unheard in the juvenile court, and many of them have been taken away from good parents and placed in bad foster care, as it happened to my children.

Indeed, their removal of my children was not necessary. There was a strong emotional bond between me and them, and I was very interested in their lives. Besides that my children had higher self-esteem, performed better in school, and were happy with me.

The juvenile judge made a superficial decision and stole my children from me without considering their interests. She didn't promote the stability and security of the family by establishing minimum standards to prevent arbitrary and unnecessary removal of my children.

The primary emphasis of the juvenile court is to keep the family intact if at all possible. This is truly what is in the best interest of the children. If it is true that juvenile court and social services are dedicated to the protection of minors, why then there are so many abuses!

No longer is a judgment based on what the child needs, with whom to be with, or what is really best for the whole family. When a child is unjustly removed by a social worker and approved by a judge, so the problem is not only related to social workers, but also to the court itself. Judges are the ones who make judgments, and the ones who establish rules and decisions.

Taking away someone's liberty and locking them up away from home, family and friends is one of the most serious decisions that can be imposed, and that can raise profound ethical questions to ones who must respond to justice.

There is no stronger trauma for a child than being deprived of their parents, especially the mother. Research indicates that keeping children away from their homes interferes with their development. The more traumatic the separation, the more likely there will be significant negative developmental consequences.

Indeed, juvenile courts in Italy do not protect children's rights. They don't help families, but they help themselves!

Fraud, coercion, extortion, and kidnapping are the procedural norm in these courts. Social workers are the glue that holds "the system" together that funds the judges and the multiple other members of the gang.

The real social worker must be a cheater and must guarantee a turnover instead of assisting families. This makes the great deal last longer than usual and Juvenile Judges want to exploit them for their own gain by making easy decrees of removal and adoption. It is a massacre and an open market where children became like sheep, and they must be sold to leave their places to other victims.

The dirty child abduction institution is the land of gang opportunity, a land of blood and money, blood and torture of the vulnerable. Dirty money is the illusory happiness of the blind. Verily, it is not the eyes that grow blind, but it is the hearts that are in the breasts that grow blind.

They are incapable of loyalty to individuals, groups, or social values. They are grossly selfish, callous, irresponsible, impulsive, and unable to feel guilt or to learn from experience. They are ready to commit all kinds of crimes; they are capable of harming, imprisoning, and even killing innocent people. They are trained to do everything for the money in the filthy institutions of madness.

Exposing my daughters to faulty psychiatry

"She cannot see her children because they are undergoing psychotherapy..." said the judge Salvatore to my lawyer. She didn't admit that separation from parents does not mean losing a home but losing a whole life. She underestimates the lives of children and views them as mere merchandise and a source of profit. Her unfair and absurd words made me feel a sharp pain in my head and completely lose faith in Italian authority. After my daughters were taken away, I wasn't allowed to see them for about a year and for no reason. This isolating indicates a scheme to brainwash them, exploit them, and then sell them.

During this period, I was doing everything I could to see them. I was extremely concerned about their health and safety; wondering what kind of people they lived with, they may feel deep sadness with strangers who don't get along with them, they may feel a loss of safety and a sense of destruction. They may be exposed to all kinds of abuse.

I hired five lawyers sequentially in order to get my two daughters back but to no avail. Even the best lawyer can do nothing. You are not allowed to hear the evidence against you. You are not able to contest any statements made by social workers whether fraudulent or not nor are you be allowed to give evidence to the contrary. The reason you are not be able to do any of those things afforded as rights of due process is because neither you, nor your lawyer is to be allowed in that courtroom.

Faced with this endless play and faced with the constant refusal to see my children. I started protesting in front of government institutions. Several Italian newspapers wrote about my protests, such as 'Cazzeta di Reggio' and 'Il Resto del Carlino' in Reggio Emilia city.

Whenever I went to the social workers to ask to see my daughters, they kicked me out. I remember once when I walked into the office of Angela Campari, the responsible or social worker in Correggio, this sadistic personality who enjoys feeling the others' pain, is a tough-tempered person, hardcore in her dealings with others, and intentionally hurt people.

She looked contemptuously at me from my feet to my head - What are you doing here? She said

"I need to see my daughters" I answered

She walked out of her office and laughed hysterically like she had an electric shock - "We didn't take anything from you." She said. A feeling of humiliation and indignity aggravated deep inside me. So, I gathered my outrage and gazed at her expectantly, incredulously refusing to accept her actions and said: you kidnapped my daughters, the core of my heart. Where did you take them?

"You must leave and don't come here again, otherwise, I will call the police." She said mockingly

I was completely stunned by her aggressive behaviour and her disregard for the lives of others; I sat in front of the social services premise, mudded, thrown into confusion. I was gathering up my jumbled senses and began to remonstrate why? What harm did I do to her to insult me in such a horrible way? Why this hatred and hostility? Why did she and her colleagues feel happy because of our sadness? Do I not possess the right to fear for my children and ask about them?

Her painful behaviour made me worried about my daughters even more; they were brought into a terrible situation. I lived through countless kinds of torment, bewilderment, and a deep-seated fear for my children's safety. I never gave up asking and fighting to get my girls back to me. The more social workers tried to stop me, the more my persistence took me to the mountains of challenge. But who can withstand the hurricane to the end?

Who can beat the rampage of the waves to the last breath?

When my file was transferred to the new social services office in Polo 3, Reggio Emilia, which was near my new residence region. I had a lot of hopes that the upcoming social workers would be humane and sympathetic. Unfortunately, winds blow counter to what ships desire.

I was disappointed when I realized that their hearts are full of wickedness, and their institution was gloomy, filled with characters who have long accepted to treat people with foxiness and betrayal. This is not alien to them since their boss, Federica Anghinolfi, is involved in serious violations. She also used to share the pie with juvenile judges when she sold the children to her lovers, homosexual, to strengthen her love affair with them.

During the interview with me, Anghinolfi and social worker Elisa Santachiara seemed cruel as they feel no sympathy for their victims. They always treated me harshly and without mercy. They both refused to allow me to see my daughters, claiming that the girls were doing psychotherapy and had to avoid meeting their parents, otherwise, the treatment would be ineffective. But who is doing this treatment, and how is it done?

It is fatal and defective psychotherapy that has been conducted by opportunists and failed psychiatrists and psychologists such as the psychologist Valeria Donati who brainwashed my daughters and adopted one of them after falsely accusing me. Children are particularly vulnerable to fraudulent, negligent, and even abusive practices.

It was a serious dilemma that they tricked me into severing my relationship with my daughters. Their misleading claims were hiding treacherous secrets of abusing them. My daughters had a close relationship with me, and not allowing them to even see me is unjustified punishment.

In this extremely painful way, they intended to make them utterly despair of returning to their natural parents, and this reflected negatively on their health. This deprivation could cut the thread of life, ways of life, and ways of psychological, mental, and emotional development of them. The real goal of preventing my little girls from seeing me was the title of a criminal plan to brainwash and sell them.

To facilitate child trafficking, the brain is not only brainwashed to erase good memories but also to generate very bad and false memories against their parents so that they believe they have been physically and sexually abused. More diabolical methods were also followed for this purpose, which were found in the judicial investigation under the code name: "Angels and Demons".

Immorality, unethicality, deception, malice, and the crisis reach its climax. This made me feel like I was at war for my blood and flesh. I have been struggling furiously all season. I did my utmost to save my children. I went on hunger strike and did a series of protests in front of government institutions in Italy and Morocco. Sadly, my voice was never heard and the suffering of my daughters was not taken into account by the authorities that stipulated child protection laws. I realized that those who set these laws are the first to break them.

The effects of these gross behaviours on the part of these institutions, which should protect people in difficulty, have harmed, and caused very serious damage to my children and me. "Angels and Demons" scandal, of which no one will forget, given the gravity of the accusations, and of the evidence gathered attesting to the terrible tragedy caused to us and our poor children, victims of these events.

The situation of my little girls can represent a collective failure, proof that the corrupt system is a great calamity to families and needs to be immediately ceased. Therefore, the question from citizens and people of goodwill arises spontaneously, where is the Judicial Authority, which perhaps has been defenestrated by this subject?

CHAPTER THREE

MY HORRIBLE INTERVIEW WITH JUVENILE JUDGE

Judge played the role of thief and cunning

Inflicting harm or pain on someone incapable of doing the same to you might seem intolerably cruel, but it happens more than you might think in juvenile courts. Disgusting and immoral acts occur in these courts and in children's social services. The unconstitutional and illegal conduct of the corrupt regime has increased dramatically throughout the most of these institutions.

I went to meet the judge Francesca Salvatore in the juvenile court of Bologna city. I had thought that she would do justice to me and so I could get my daughters back easily, after everything seemed to be in order:
I hired a lawyer to claim my daughters back. I also broke up with my violent ex-husband, and I had a permanent job and a decent house.

The day I went to court was a very sad day like every day I spent on my own after the absence of my children. Just as a running after a mirage, I led a meaningless, worthless life. Endless days and nights of longing that burns my heart and invades my soul. Memories rose up to take me back to the cursed separation moment. The moment of assault and injustice that still haunts me.

In the juvenile court, I was sitting idly by while the judge was slamming at me with harsh words. Words fell like a sword on my heart, painful memories and deception that cannot be forgotten!

The court was so quite depressing. The causes of this depression were also sad where loved ones, children, and grandchildren were lost. The sad memories are followed by the groans of persecuted parents and children killed alive. What a dramatic and miserable court! It deprives you from everything and then turns you down, imprison you if you don't obey it or if you don't surrender to its grim reality.

Thousands of false decrees were stored in the archives of the Tribunal, and numbered acts were hung on its walls; contained many of the promises denied by their founders.

I asked a receptionist that I would like to speak with the judge Salvatore

"She's in a meeting, you should wait for her." He replied

I gave my name and sat waiting impatiently for the judge to come. I was obsessed and confused, wondering what her response would be.

After an hour, Salvatore showed up and looked skinny with ruthless features. While sneaking into her office, she was peeking at the guests just like a thief does when he is afraid to get caught. She entered her office and slammed the door behind her which caused me considerable dismay.

It sounded like a wake-up call to tell me that there was no room for argument. Despite that, I didn't lose hope, and I felt that my heart flew to her office to argue with her. I rushed to the office door to knock.

"Step inside please" She said

I came in, greeted her, and stood still while she cast a rough look at me. "How can I help you?" She asked firmly.

"I seek your permission to return my daughters to me"
I replied.

"The children are no longer yours and will not be recovered." She responded sarcastically

I was dominated by a severe turmoil. I got furious and felt as tightness was suffocating my soul; "But My daughters are in desperate need of me, and this deprivation will cause profound harm to them" I said

"I don't have time to talk." She replied

"I want to know the reason for this dangerous act that you are doing and depriving my daughters of me. What is the reason behind that?"

"Don't ask a lot of questions. Leave, please." She said.

Certainly, they do not have time, as every new becomes old once it is traded. The ending of the conversation had dashed any hope of peace. My spring of hope was in a superlative degree of silent fade. Her harsh actions were hiding economic interests and planning to sell my daughters.

This is an Illegal profit on the skins of the weak as souls are killed and bodies are shrouded, and buried in endless depths, in the utmost secrecy and with cold blood. It is the age of darkness and widespread corruption within the government departments!!

I left the court, broken, confused, disappointed, and in floods of tears. I found myself on a dark route. There was sleet, snow, and heart frost. I was left alone all the time when sadness attacked me, alone facing the world, alone facing the cruelty and brutality of these acts of torture that defy description. Their cruelty can shatter everything like fire when burning firewood. They have no conscience at all about destroying families as their feelings have dried up.

How hard it is to deal with people whose hearts are like rocks, even tougher! Rivers burst from rocks, but all sorts of evils burst from their hearts.

I couldn't believe that even the judge ignored me and did not grant me justice. Even the judge eats human flesh and feeds her children with this flesh that belongs to them; flesh of innocents like them. This judge made me lose faith in the judiciary. She caused me fear, suffering and humiliation –these are violations of human dignity.

I left the court; I was spinning in a vortex around the streets of Reggio Emilia and Bologna cities, and between juvenile court and social services like foliage when autumn storms sway them left and right, wandering in the alleys in search of my precious daughters. They were lost just as the little things are lost among the big things. They were lost just as pets are lost among predators. They are human wolves that are more deadly and fierce than real wolves, with their reckless instincts, their persistence in de-civilization, and their disavowal of morals and humanity.

To what extent is depriving a child of their family a priority in relation to his mental and physical health, or a solution that determines the quality of life for all family members? And is this decision consistent with the local and international law on children's rights?

Law no. 184 of 1983 (entitled Right of the minor to a family) governs the institution of family custody, which aims to remedy situations of temporary incapacity of parents exercising parental responsibility, which hinder the right of the minor to his own family. To this end, the law provides for support and help interventions in favour of the family of origin.

Foster care, according to Italian law, is a tool aiming at protecting the minor, which has a fixed duration and which can end either in a return to the family of origin or in the declaration of the state of adoptability when the parents are no longer able to fulfill the function of parental.

The factual circumstances that deprive the minor of a suitable family environment may concern the personality of the parent (serious behavioral deficiencies, illnesses, etc.)

None of the reasons that could lead to putting my daughters up for adoption apply to me. I had decent housing and a permanent job, I broke up with the violent husband, and I had no mental illness

The period of presumed duration of the assignment must be indicated in the provision of custody, which must be attributable to the interventions aimed at the recovery of the child to his family of origin. But, in my case, I was deceived and unjustly deprived of my daughters.

I was judged as incompetent while I was doing all my best to protect my children. A mother who possesses positive qualities and protective components is capable of reducing anxiety and worries, and a figure that has a sentimental attachment to her children is capable to respond adequately to their emotional. Unfortunately, the juvenile judge Francesca Salvatore made arbitrary decisions; removed my children from a good mother and subjected them to punishment.

This is a great trauma, and an appalling tragedy that struck me and my children. I found myself childless in a few hours oppressively. It is infinite cruelty and inhuman treatment.

This judge perpetrated injustice and did not order verification of my parenting skills. She also treated my case superficially without contributing to the analysis of the issue or the identifying possible solutions.

It's all because she thinks about her own interests and doesn't take into consideration children's needs and welfare. This judge, notorious with her colleagues for corruption and child trafficking, did not take my case to hearings and did not provide any factual justification.

The real purpose of taking away my children was a plan to sell them through the illegal adoption procedure. Judge Salvatore had abused her authority, went out of her way to separate children and mother and to terminate parental rights. She kept my two daughters in a "protracted foster care," and then sold them in a scheme of illegal adoption.

Salvatore was at best negligent, and at worst intentional when she "did everything in her power" to rip my children off me with no regard for their rights. She took a punitive approach towards me and my little girls, focusing more on taking them away than prioritizing their needs or providing services to alleviate our problems.

Salvatore also refused to allow my parents to communicate with my children when they traveled to

Italy and stayed there for 3 years. Salvatore assaulted my daughters and deprived them of their parents, grandparents, and relatives without cause, without warrants or justification.

Judge Salvatore hasn't changed the direction of difficulty. She has made the problem bigger, and she took her lead to torture my children and destruct them. Her arbitrary decision to deprive my daughters of their parents, grandparents, and relatives reveals child confiscation, forced adoption, and heavy losses due to theft and fraud in the juvenile court. It is appalling that Juvenile Judges see a justifiable reason to take a child from their birth parents because fosters are available.

Juvenile Judge's task is to secure contracts for care centers to house stolen children, and these centers must be kept filled. When every child is sold, it must be replaced by another new one immediately. Juvenile Judges, seeking to satisfy consumer demand, and guarantee billions of euros each year. Those dirty Euros, too often, induce the unscrupulous judges and their followers to defraud, coerce, and kidnap children away from their beloved families. Corrupt 'Children for Cash' judges ruined more than five hundred thousand lives.

Oh judge, what punishment does you and those who deceived us deserve? You deluded us with help and made us swallow up bitter disappointments. What sanction do you all merit on those wounds that you planted in our depths?

What price is that can cure the scars that can't be healed.

Do you know how many kinds of torment that you have inflicted on our children? How long will the hearts of our children still cry out in silence, and nobody is willing to answer these bleeding hearts?

Breaking the law of the United Nations

Child has the right to live with their natural parents as long as these parents are fit and don't expose them to danger. UN law prohibits illegal adoption and criminalizes child abduction, child trafficking, child prostitution, child pornography, and any illegal activity or practice such as lack of proper consent by biological parents and illegitimate profit by mediators. Falsification of official documents, coercion and the associated corruption constitute illegal adoptions must be prohibited, criminalized, and punished with penalties that reflect the gravity of the crimes. UN law also recognizes the right of motherhood and childhood to "special protection and assistance" and the right of all children to social protection. Illegal adoptions violate many child rights norms and principles including the best interests of the child. These principles are violated when the purpose of the adoption is to find a child for the adoptive parents as an alternative custody and trafficking of children which leads to illegal adoption.

If we reconsider what is happening in the Italian juvenile courts right now, we discover that the rights sanctioned by the United Nations are absent and subverted. Such actions are gross violations of human rights and contrary to the international law. We are dealing with a series of human rights violations which, in turn, mask conflict of interest between Juvenile Judges, social services, politics, psychiatrists and psychologists. We see more propaganda proliferated that supports social workers.

These criminally intentioned aggressors find lucrative means to obtain their victims through already corrupted social services processes. The masked adoption is daily bread for them! The terms illegal adoption and racketeering are often used by the mass media to indicate certain phenomena related to the trade in children.

Social service institutions and the juvenile court system in which they work are secreted away, self-investigating, and exist under laws and limitations of criminal prosecution that violate the laws and statutes of the nation. They pay themselves off and can act without limit.

As a parent, I condemn the perpetrators of that heinous act and I raise a question: Why does not the United Nations intervene rigorously to put an end to all these blatant abuses? How is a child with a living family transformed into a "paper orphan," adopted for someone else's profit? Their lives have been scarred by corrupt adoptions. What Italian policy changes might prevent children from being wrongfully taken from their birth families, simultaneously helping to stop creating orphans instead of saving the vulnerable ones?

CHAPTER FOUR

HEART-BREAKING MEETINGS WITH MY CHILDREN

Weird rules during the meetings

After one year of suffering and struggling, I was allowed to see my daughters for just few times, and I had to apply weird rules during protective meetings; listen and obey-like a slave. I found out that my older daughter lived in foster care family in mountainous area, and my younger daughter lived in child foster institute, 'Cenacolo Francescano', where the protecting meeting would be.

Before the first meeting, I was called by the social worker Elisa Santachiara to come to her office at Polo 3 in Reggio Emilia. And through the interview, she created opinions and positions that had nothing to do with reality. She began to dictate odd rules that I had to apply during the protected meetings with my children:

"Listen and open your ears well;"

"Don't kiss them more than once in each meeting."

"Don't hug them or tell them that you love them"

"Don't remind them of anything related to the past"

"Don't talk to them about their grandparents or their relatives"

"Don't give them a promise to come back to you."

She added with malicious joy:

"This is a court order, and all you have to do is to play with them until the time allowed is up."

I was hit hardly by what I had heard. It was beyond belief and too much for human patience.
They wanted us to play a game, a game that represents their tricks; we are only a game in their hands.

I could not believe what she was saying, the phrases choked in my throat, lowered my head, and my eyes turned tears. I listened to my emotions, and it tortured me.
How can I stand up to these sordid rules?
How can I become a body without a soul?
When I give my children hope to return to live with me, will it harm them?
If I tell them I love you, would that harm them?

Diabolical plan behind the strange rules

I know that motherhood cannot be suppressed by unjust rules or oppressive laws. The real purpose behind these rules is that they intend to make my relationship with my children superficial, devoid of feelings and tenderness that consolidate the bonds between mother and children. These rules will generate a false image in the children's brains that their mother is indifferent to them, abandoned them, and doesn't care about their needs; thus, children will lose a sense of safety because the true reference to them, the mother, has become indifferent to their interests.

Conclusively, they want to make my daughters feel excluded, not enjoy their mother's love. Neglecting them physically or emotionally can affect them in an extremely negative way. Neglect is a very common type of child abuse, and it can be as harmful as physical abuse. Ignoring the needs of my children or making them feel worthless can cause low self-esteem, and even life-long psychological scars.

A child needs to feel loved and cherished. Preventing me from communicating with my children and making it clear to them that I love and value them, can lead to an unstable relationship that makes it easier for social workers, psychologists, and psychiatrists to carry out their criminal acts, which are the submission of my little girls to brainwashing, and shaping their behaviours as they want.

Meetings with my children

How do social services become a truncheon in the hands of executioners? Cursed are those institutions whose professionals fight love and kill the meaning of motherhood which is the best blessing in life. They crush warm relationships with our children, shatter our feelings, and break our hearts.

They make our children become our enemies and turn them into a heartless profit machine. They charge them every day with what they have to say and do, beware that if children do not do what they have been taught, they will be subjected to all kinds of psychological and physical punishment. That's what I have learned from the protected encounters with my daughters.

When the day of the first appointment came, I bought many gifts and all the things that my daughters love. I gladdened to see my daughters, but I did not know that other troubles were waiting for me. Especially since I was not comfortable with the rules imposed on me.

High walls, gloomy souls, cuffed freedom, streamed tears, and oppressed innocence. This is the reality of the child foster institute "Cenacolo Francescano." I rang the bell and after a few minutes, a nun showed up carrying keys in her hand. She looked plump and man-like in her haircut, dress, and way of walking. She opened the door and asked me to come in. I greeted her then I walked behind her.

I remarked that the courtyard garden was as barren as the hearts of the children living behind its walls. Innocent hearts deprived of their loved ones, groaned, hurt by words, scarred by the memory of separation, and prematurely marred and lost in wild darkness without their tormentors feeling their pain, and no one listening to their complaints.

A lamp lit up and a room looked narrow, square patch. I sat on a chair waiting for my daughters. Suddenly, the social worker Santachiara and the educator Chiara Rabboni came with my daughters, who as soon as they saw me ran and fell into my arms, hugging me.

It was joy mixed with pain, my daughters cried heartily; feeling fear, loss and confusion that they had never felt before. They were under abnormal pressure and stress that was caused by major aggressive behaviours and by a series of abuses and irritations of social workers, educators, psychologists, and psychiatrists.

I embraced my little girls and was overcome with tears that poured out of my eyes. I tried to calm my daughters and asked them what happened:

My daughter Chaymae complained bitterly: "Mum, we were told that you had abandoned us, why?"

"That's absolutely not true, I'm waging war to bring you live with me" I replied

"I was molested, please help me, and take me away from here as soon as possible." She said

My younger daughter Fatma was crying a lot,

"They beat me Mum, they force me to take a freeze shower, I feel hungry every day, I dream wolves eating me, I can't live there anymore, Mum help me" She said

In the face of these shocking confessions, the two social workers were provoked as their dirty secrets had come out. "We have to end the meeting because you haven't followed the rules" said Santachiara.

They wanted to make me look like a dupe and as if nothing happened. They scolded us because we didn't respect the rules without taking into account our feelings and pains. This is coercion and swallowing the overwhelming bitterness!

I blamed myself for requesting help from this criminal organisation that called itself "social workers." I wished if I had resolved my problem alone, and all these misfortunes would not have happened. I was distraught with grief and remorse and wished that I would be pulled towards the middle of the sea and pushed into the depths.

I took my daughters in my arms, and with a loud cry I attacked the social workers: "Let my little girls come with me, criminals" The two social workers started quarreling with me, and some nuns hurried to the room, and they all pulled my daughters from my lap fiercely.

Social workers threatened my children, abused them, and forced them to live in foster care which is beyond their ability. That was being very damaging to their well-being, and juvenile judge does not criminalize these atrocities.

How my children could be immediately ignored when they expressed their will to return to normal life and be able to live with their mother? They manipulated them in return and trampled their true needs.

Abuse of my daughters in foster care

The next meeting appointment was delayed for six months due to my daughter's broken arm. A social worker called me before the meeting, and I thought the date would be fixed, but winds blow counter to what ships desire.

She said: Your daughter Fatma has broken her arm and can only be seen after a few months.

I said: What caused the breakage? She ignored my question, I continue speaking nervously: My daughter needs me more now, I must meet her

She said: it is not possible now.

I was furious over what happened to my daughter.

I contacted Reggio Emilia Hospital, paediatric ward, and they informed me that my daughter, Fatma, was recovered twice there for a broken arm.

I went on a hunger strike for several days, and I protested in front of Reggio Emilia municipal and social service premise. Several newspapers wrote about my case.

My daughter's arm was broken due to abuse from the educator Rabboni. I am asking the authorities for the truth and justice for these abuses. According to the rule (art.33 **law 833/78)** "during the compulsory medical treatment, the sick person has the right to communicate with anyone they deem appropriate"

These violent methods would evoke deportation to a concentration camp more than hospitalisation. Social workers postponed meetings between me and my daughters, denying the necessity of these meetings when my younger daughter's arm was broken, and preventing her from emotional support from her mother which could help her feel better.

But social workers did the opposite and increased my daughter's torment while she was having a hard time feeling comfortable and dealing with pain, while she was having a stressful and upsetting experience, suffering from serious fracture.

They were not only prevented my children from seeing me, but also from seeing their grandparents, who came from Morocco to visit them. Under threat and mistreatment, as the medical records show- in Reggio Emilia city Hospital, paediatric ward, on the criminal behaviour of these social workers. The law should have stopped them, and this didn't quite happen, and they continued to torture my children.

When the next protected meeting appointment arrived after long months, I found out my daughters' behaviour became strange, they had not remained cheery and happy as they were. They looked pale and gloomy, which expressed a clear image of the abuse they were suffering; in their tones sounds a deeper pain mixed with fear. They were so happy to see me, but the existence of the social workers changed safety to fear and happiness to sadness.

My younger daughter Fatma was at the height of her agony, tension, and confusion after the incident, her arm had a lot of stitches and looked as if it was struck by a sharp object. I asked her: Who broke your arm Fatma?

She cried a lot and pointed her finger at the educator Chiara Rabboni and said: "She hit me with a stick many times and broke my arm." I was frightened and enraged, and my eyes blurred with tears of outrage. I was practically screaming with my growing frustration which made me a bitter woman.

"Don't be ashamed of abusing my daughter in such a brutal manner? I said to Rabboni:

"You are not allowed to talk about anything relating the children, the judge entrusted them to us." She shuddered and replied.

I felt the air was slowly lacking and the ground narrowed more and more. It was almost like our lives collapsing quietly and nobody can save them. The social workers were playing the assassins as if they were pointing a weapon at us and they decided to kill us in cold blood.

I was terrified, by their extreme cruelty and abuses. My children were exposed to physical violence and verbal abuse. They indeed suffered aggression, all sorts of abuses, and were spanked and slurred which inflicted psychological damage as well. Despite all this, judges don't want me to defend my daughters. Nobody wants me to defend my daughters. Even when I complained to the Italian Parliament and Ministry of Justice, they ordered the police to expel me.

They said to me, "Shut your mouth, and don't attack." But there is nothing that can stop me from defending my children! I am ready to give my life for them.

I looked like someone with a sword to defeat enemies to fight for my daughters to save them from the unexpected terror they lived in.

During this meeting, social workers, enemies of humanity were unbelievably gloating over my daughter's pain as she was still suffering her arm fracture. Every now and then, they were looking stealthily; winking with each other, and from time to time a wide smile ran on their lips, a mocking smile, as a delivered message of some memories of their criminal acts. They wage war against us and spread mischief in the land. They didn't care about our feelings, they treated us as slaves. They wanted to crucify us or exiled us from the land. They really are devil soldiers!

In fact, people without souls can lie, cheat, rape, and murder to get what they want. These are the people to whom the state pays MORE money to ATTACK our children. This is stigmatization and disgrace that no honest person or any responsible with a living conscience accepts. This is a disgrace to the authority that maintains a deadly silence that kills our children every day.

Meeting in the holiday house in Marina di Massa

The massive violence against my children was not over yet. In Massa Marina di Carrara city, a largest affiliate of "Cenacolo San Francescano" foster institute is located, where children brought there on holidays.

The meeting appointment with my children was booked there. So, it was a long journey that took about four hours to arrive, I took with me, as usual, many gifts and everything my daughters loved. I found out that this institute was grimy and isolated like a desert, extremely large like a prison hiding behind its walls statues of ice of children killed by life. Despite of its vastness, it was a narrow place, testified to the greatest tragedy that could happen in history.

I had rung the bell, and after about fifteen minutes came the same nun that was working in Reggio Emilia section. But this time she didn't open the door, she was bothered by my presence, and she was so confused. Then she spoke to me from behind the gate. "Come back in two hours please," I delivered all the gifts to her from above the wall to delight my daughters with my presence.

I didn't know where to go because I had never been there before, I noticed that there was a small cafe nearby, I sat there but I didn't rest, I came back watching what was going on around this institute. What caught my attention was the arrival of too many guests; of course, they were not all parents especially since some of them looked homosexual by their physical appearance, which made me feel like something abnormal was happening.

At four o'clock the gate was opened for me, I saw my daughters slipped out from socials workers, their eyes shone with joy, and they ran towards me, hugged me and the moment was plenty of hugs and smiles. Suddenly, they were freaked out by the shouting of two social workers that was coming from afar, muttering frightening insults because of my little girls' behaviour.

Their words fell on my heart like a thunderbolt, and I almost burst into anger because of their sharp tongues, But I did not want to respond to them at that moment, out of respect for my daughters' feelings. Their insults, orders, and reprimands which made me feel that there was more serious abuse against my daughters. For that I was deeply fearful for my daughters' safety.

We sat in an underground room. I cuddled with my daughters, hold their hands, and said that I love them so much. They felt great happiness, and soon the scene became full of emotions and warm with love, which arouse social workers who looked at us with indignation.

They ate the cake that I gave on Chaymae' s birthday, they liked it and the gifts. Chaymae's birthday would be after two days, but I used this meeting as an opportunity to celebrate it. I gave hope to my daughters that their future birthdays will be with me at home.

"This should not be said, because it would not be true". Said Santachiara

My little girls were stunned and burst in tears.

They always spoil our happiness even within an hour of meeting. It seemed that they were accustomed to tyranny and torturing others. My daughters' crying was making them happy and elated. Their evil souls appeared and incited them to enjoy tormenting others. It was as a result of sadism illness where seductive thoughts occupied their minds.

I calmed my children down and said with challenge "We will celebrate birthdays at home, do not believe them." Social workers had looked at me with disgust, and then Rabboni with her long nails that resembled the claws of an eagle, grabbed both of my daughters savagely to the point that they cried out in pain, and had left with them before the allowed time was over.

I felt as if life stopped at that unexpected moment. I left, broken as usual, thinking about these fangs of human wolves that tore our hearts. I came back home disappointed, shocked by my daughter's miserable conditions, and by those damn rules that restricted their souls, their tongues, and even their feelings. The fear that the girls suffered in my presence from these criminals was only a small part of what they were experiencing in my absence.

They didn't know what was really happening because their minds couldn't comprehend all of these problems. It is beyond incredible that social workers instead of strengthening the relationship between parent and child, they ruin it! The abuse of children by social services has a detrimental effect on their physical mental and emotional well-being, and consequently a harmful effect on their future. Despite all the violations, social workers continue their practices without any accountability.

CHAPTER FIVE

UNFAIR JUDGMENT AGAINST ME

The medical records deny the false report

I remember once when an Italian lawyer said to me, "Many innocent people are in prison." I was stunned by what I heard. I never imagined that the end of my story could be such a tragedy centred on these words.

Not everyone who is punished is truly guilty. There are victims who do not deserve to be punished because they have nothing to do with the legal scenes, and there are victims at a tender age.

In 2009, the head of Social Services Federica Anghinolfi, who is one of the main characters involved in a series of crimes against children and parents in the investigation of "Angels and Demons," decided that my daughters could not be brought back either to my house or to my parents' house, and no further meetings will be organized.

At that point, I became insistent, exhausted by this vicious calumny that made my blood boil, and made me look like a person completely different from reality. For this reason, I got mad at the social workers; I showed up at public offices to protest and went on hunger strike. Of course, this didn't help my case, but I had no other remedies because what was happening was absurd and destructive.

Subsequently, something weird happened and changed everything: I was accused of abusing my daughters and making them prostitute. When, however, from 2006 to 2009 no one talked about sexual abuse. They only talked about parental incapacity!! This was the first unjustified accusation.

Despite this, the picture began to change as Anghinolfi together with the Psychologist Valeria Donati, asserted before the judicial authority that the girls reported that their mother had forced them to prostitution, therefore social workers blocked everything, suspending the protected mother/daughters' encounters.

In 2009 their colleague Dr. Maria Stella D'Andrea wrote a report that she had a gynecological examination on my two daughters, using the tools (colposcope, camera, cotton swab), and that she concluded that the girls were subjected to sexual violence, and this is part of her report `` The girls have been subjected to acts of sexual violence, carried out by vaginal penetration of a hard-elastic medium and with the use of physical force"

If the girls were sexually abused as you claim, then who raped them? Doctors, in 2006, examined the girls, using the same tools you used, confirmed they had "intact genitals" and they were not sexually abused; these doctors did not report any attributable injuries to abuse of a sexual nature. Also I was present with the girls during the medical examination, in 2006 at a hospital in Guastalla, where we stayed for three days. Since all of this is true then who abused my daughters?

And why was your medical visit of 2010 inconsistent with medical visits of 2006? And since 2006 my daughters have not lived with me, and they never came back to my house. So how can they be sexually abused in 2010?! All these false accusations only arose out of nowhere after four years! Since the girls had never said anything about it before, and still, the same medical reports of 2006 DO NOT REPORT ANY SEXUAL VIOLENCE EXPERIENCED. But coincidentally it was reported later after four years that they had suffered sexual violence. Keeping in mind that they were not even placed with me, but at the social service to which they had been entrusted, (that is, the older daughter was placed in a foster family, and the younger daughter was placed in the Cenacolo Francescano, the foster institute of Reggio Emilia.

These criminals use dangerous methods and anesthesia for children to abuse them. How it could not be you who have subjected my daughters to sexual abuse and other abuses and want to blame me after manipulating their minds. So much so that all the evidence indicates that these violations that she claims occurred when my daughters started living away from me and all medical certificates were done after 2006, after four years.

This gang rape children and criminalize their parents to cover up their crimes and escape punishment, but they did not know they would fall for the trap, as their medical certificates in 2010 contradict medical certificates in 2006 forgetting my presence and my knowledge of these certificates of 2006.

They violated the principles of the scientific method by testifying about events that were never conducted, suppressing evidence, misinterpreting results, and using tricks to camouflage the reality. This indicates their manipulation of many people's souls and lives.

Personal injury, sexual violence against minors, child pornography, grooming are serious crimes, committed by them while pretending to protect children, committed to the detriment of minors; these are crimes that inflict not only physical violence on the minor, but also and above all psychological violence which is difficult to overcome and which can mark their entire existence.

The investigation, which has its roots in the summer of 2018 and continues to this day and whose protagonist was Anghinolfi, has shown that the children have been abused in every way. It emerged that psychologists and social workers wanted to make money by taking advantage of the fostering of children: once mentally manipulated, they were entrusted to other families, who would profit from the funds. Psychologists, on the other hand, would made money from therapy sessions.

This accusation was inconsistent with the medical examinations, the indisputable evidence that the doctors carried out in 2006 and issued from Guastalla Hospital, stated that the girls did not suffer any injuries attributable to maltreatment of a sexual nature.

The medical records confirmed that: ‘‘BOTH GIRLS’GENITALS ARE INTACT’’– and since 2006 my daughters have not lived with me; they were strapped by social workers, and they haven’t come back to my home. So how can they be victims of sexual abuse in 2009?!

When I started practising pressures to get my daughters back, then, at this point, I was accused oppressively of maltreatments that never happened from me. And again, how could they be subjected to sexual abuse, while the medical certificates in 2006 confirmed: that both of "the girls' genital parts are intact!?"

These medical reports are strong evidence that raise serious question about the integrity of the judges who unjustly sentenced me for crimes I had not committed. This case highlights the issues surrounding wrongful many parents’ convictions in prison across the country.

Another thing must be taken into consideration, four years after brainwashing my daughters into believing they had been abused, four years after dozens and dozens of unregistered private sessions to build negative effects on them and to make improper suggestions to them, four years after changing their memories, spoiling their feelings, and ruining my reputation in their eyes. After that all, they mentioned that the girls said that they were abused!!

It was a cruel irony and an absurd new episode. It was the voice of mockery, the act of criminality. This is not only outside the law, but also outside logic and out of mind. It was not built on scientific basis. It was built on falseness and deception, for they are indeed great deceptive people. Their heads contain all sorts of evil, "Hmm if we don't accuse parents, then how can we kidnap children, how can we sell them, and how can we easily make a fortune?"

It is obvious that their inner selves represent what they really are on the inside. Their purposes, their values, their visions, their motivations, their goals, and their beliefs are false. Everything is false–such opportunists people are given the lead to protect children! Storm of lies and atrocious cruelties!

It was also outside humanity, ripping my daughters–ripping my heart, and afterwards, accusing me falsely. This was a plan to sell my daughters in adoption scheme. These responsible people, instead of helping my daughters and me, they destroyed us. I had been thrown into the criminal court system and found myself in "you are guilty."

I have struggled with deep anxiety, fear, and despair. A feeling of intense injustice came over me and began to oppress and torture my heart. I had, by now, reached such a pitch, and had taken such a definite form, that I did not know what to do with myself to escape from my great sorrow. I didn't know how to stand up to this injustice. I didn't know how to struggle this oppression. I have fought to navigate a war that never ending. I did everything I could, but it was inevitably doomed to fail.

Just imagine how you would handle having your children removed and having to deal with false allegations to which you had no recourse! Nothing should be introduced as evidence unless it is proven and documented. Our lives are at stake, and this is not the place for hearsay and assumptions. It was not enough for them to deprive me of my daughters, and the pain and grief that I live in, they also accused me and sentenced me unjustly.

The judge condemns me despite my innocence

A judge may issue a decree of imprisonment against an innocent, just as they wash their faces in the morning, and that is because an accusation is made by social workers, no matter if it is false. Indeed, a lot of social workers are friends of judges; I saw some of them with my own eyes sitting at a court cafe, joking and giggling– perhaps among these jokes were a gloat over misfortune people that they had been sentenced unjustly.

The Judge Andrea Scarpa, at the Criminal Court of Bologna, in 2011 sentenced me in absentia without considering the evidence, and he judged me without looking at the irrefutable arguments that prove my innocence, indeed, he used what his colleagues, psychologists and social workers provided to indict me unfairly. This judge deliberately destroyed the evidence of social workers crimes. As a result, I was permanently prevented from seeing my children and having important news about them.

Are professions of virtue killed by their unscrupulous owners? If so, then who is responsible for all this, and why are the officials silent? Silence is a sign of their approval, and this approval has only one reason, which is to share the profit with those vices that have betrayed their professions and people.

In the face of these absurd abuses, I made several complaints to Italian parliament, the court of justice in

Rome, the Italian embassy in Rabat, the Ministry of Foreign Affairs in Morocco, and the EU court of human rights in Strasbourg. Many newspapers wrote about these events.

The fact that all due process, human Rights are violated and manipulated by corrupt court judges, social services, psychologists, psychiatrists, and educators, who incriminate us, falsify documents in court, and lie in a court setting.

Social workers can lie and manufacture evidence, and they are immune from prosecution. They have no oversight, accountability or consequences. In my case, they falsely accused me because they intended to justify the kidnapping and the adoption of my daughters. They wanted my parental rights to be terminated, and I might never see my children again. The cold hard facts are these situations that destroyed our lives.

Waiting for the social workers and the psychologists to try to inculcate in the innocent minds of the little ones that they have been mistreated by their parents, every slightest pretext becomes proof of abuse that has never occurred, and from innocent white sheets, they build paper castles inhabited by artfully created monsters.

Stories are created to make money on children's skin and carry on a battle in the name of a sick ideology.

This is how the "demons" of social services in Reggio Emilia city, have set up the system of illicit custody and illicit adoption of my daughters and other children.

To those judges who unjustly deprived me of my daughters, and sentenced me to prison:

Have you understood what happens in Bibbiano (Reggio Emilia)? Have you understood the ex-responsible of social services, Federica Anghinolfi, who accused me and sold my little girls, was the boss of the gang?

Do you understand that they take children away from their families, accusing the parents of abuses that are invented from scratch, and give children in foster care to sex shops and gay couples? Do you understand that they subject them to electric shocks to manipulate their memories?

Who has falsified the drawings to substantiate the accusations? Who has failed to deliver letters and gifts given by birth parents to children?
Do you understand that the PD is in solidarity with the arrested Mayor? Do you understand that for 20 years, without anyone lifting a finger, thousands of children have been brainwashed, taken from their families, kept in foster care and subjected to a paid private care circuit?

Do you know that the psychologist Valeria Donati, who accused me and adopted my younger daughter, is involved in serious crimes over children and parents? Do you know the money funneled to municipals and Child Protective Services, are actually encourages this gang to accuse parents of child abuse and even murder, and to remove their children, even there is absolutely no proof that parents harmed them?

Oh judges, who condemned me oppressively, you know all this very well, but you still make sentences unjustly because you are involved with them in these crimes; many proofs demonstrate that, and this following report as an example, provided by the Tgr of Emilia Romagna:
"***New shocking elements have emerged in the investigation into custody in the province of Reggio Emilia.***
According to which the former manager and social worker of the social services of the Val d'Enza union, Federica Anghinolfi and Francesco Monopoli, would even have made other operators believe that in the province of Reggio Emilia there was a network of paedophiles who practised satanic rites, murders and even ritual cannibalism. Therefore, children at risk had to be removed from their families even at the cost of falsifying the reports on them.

This macabre picture would emerge from the interrogations to which the social workers were subjected: it was, specifically, a very powerful organisation which also included MAGISTRATES, law enforcement officers, professionals. Something disconcerting that has shocked the country and beyond."

The whole process of the illegal adoption is controlled directly by the state (Juvenile Judges and magistrates) and by the public administration / services (ASL, CIM, social workers, psychologists, psychiatrists etc.)

Falsifying a document is usually done in connection with broader criminal aims; a person must have acted with criminal intent.

So social workers and their psychologists acted with intent to deceive my children and me. They used fabricated statements to influence a target's beliefs by considering me as a criminal. No compelling evidence was presented to the court!

The admission of evidence pursuant to art. 261 c.p.c, is in fact left from the beginning to the definitive sentence. The ruling is, therefore, erroneous because it is based on fraud and incorrect foundations and for having rejected with insufficient motivation the further admission of logical evidence and medical examinations of 2006.

I complained about the professionals who assault my children and me, and for all their fraudulent behaviours that breached a number of human rights:

The head of the CAB **VALERIA DONATI**, the Educator **CHIARA RABBONI**, the psychologist - Psychotherapist **DANIELA CASSANELLI** of the Social Service " Cenacolo Francescano institution" of Reggio Emilia, as well as **FEDERICA ANGHINOLFI** and **ELISA SANTACHIARA** of the Social Service of the Municipality of Reggio Emilia "Personal Services Area - Territorial Social Services - Polo 3", the Judge Rapporteur **FRANCESCA SALVATORE** of the

Juvenile Court of Bologna, the judge, ANDREA SCARPA, of the criminal court of Bologna, as well as against all professionals/operators/that dealt with the affair and were responsible for the following crimes:

***Art. 481 of the criminal code 'Ideological falsehood in certificates committed by people carrying out a service of public need'**

* **Art. 374 bis of the Criminal Code 'False statements to the judicial authority'.**
* **Art. 323 of the criminal code 'Abuse of office'.**
* **Art. 368 of the criminal code 'Slander'.**
* **Art. 643 of the criminal code 'Circumvention of Incapable'.**
* **Art. 416 of the criminal code 'Criminal Association'.**
* **Art. 81 of the criminal code 'Continuation'.**
* **Art. 110 of the criminal code 'Competition of Persons in the Offence';** and for all those crimes that can be recognized in the facts as in the narrative exposed. These serious crimes are indicative of their aggression and the degeneration of their motives of domination, perversion, corruption, vilifications, slavery to money and treachery of the people.

I acquire an investigation of the juvenile court in Bologna as well as criminal court, and most important I ask that my file and my children file, social workers files, and court tapes, be put into the investigation, as well as the medical reports of my daughters so that no tampering of these documents can be done by such institutions.

CHAPTER SIX

CRIMINAL ORGANIZATION ACCUSES ME AND ADOPTS MY DAUGHTERS

Valeria Donati, Federica Anghinolfi / The terrifying truth of these characters

Among the people who kidnapped my children and wrongly accused me, the former head of social services Federica Anghinolfi, involved in the scandal of 'Bibbiano' Northern Italy, and the psychologist Valeria Donati who subjected the former children of the 'Bassa Modenese' to psychotherapy - removed at an early age from their parents who were accused for paedophilia. Today these children deny that they were abused. Only some of them, now adults, have the courage to publicly say that they were never victims of abuse.

Valeria Donati

How is it possible for a woman who accuses me to adopt my child?! The psychologist Valeria Donati used to work for the child foster institution, 'Cenacolo Francescano', and was responsible for child help centre in Reggio Emilia. This psychologist, along Federica Anghinolfi destroyed my life and life of my children. Donati, after had falsely accused me, she adopted my younger daughter, who still lives with her right now. My older daughter, instead, has been adopted by a couple who live near this psychologist's home.

What is the Article that can give the permission to such a psychologist to practise harmful behaviours towards me and my children? How can the juvenile court allow her to adopt my daughter after she had written false reports against me? How is possible for someone who sent the mother to prison to adopt her daughter?

Isn't this a very serious offense to a minor?! Aren't these heinous crimes against families? Where is the role of the authority that claims to protect the minor? Where is the role of the officials who always say the child has priority? These flagrant violations of human rights express blatant complicity and conflict of interests at the expense of the weak and vulnerable.

As a mother who has been deprived of her children and was wrongly accused, I ask for urgent intervention against this psychologist who still refuses to interpret her wrong behaviour up to now. When the press asked her to justify her adoption of my daughter and to explain the false accusations against me, she replied: "These matters are private, and I'm unable to answer" How silly is this!

How do you kidnap people's children and say these are personal things? How can this be a personal thing? Are you the one who carried my daughters, each, nine months in your womb? Are you the one who endured the pains of childbirth to see the joy in their eyes? Are you the one who breastfed my daughters, each, for two consecutive years? Are you the one who stayed up long nights for their comfort when they were babies? How can you say these are PERSONAL things?

Shame on you! Where is your conscience and where is your humanity?! You are belittling the law by saying so. You are underselling yourself as a psychologist and criminalizing psychology as well. This is the time to raise the curtain on all your illegal acts. The disgraceful actions that all of you have done against my daughters for sixteen years must be rejected and you must all be prosecuted. Criminals must not go unpunished and the justice must be done. Long-hidden crimes must be revealed to the world.

It is absolutely necessary for me to have the opportunity to communicate with my daughters so that they will be able to know the truth. For the sake of my children who have suffered so much, the competent authority should take note of the abuses being committed against them and me. My children are deprived of serenity and compelled to live with those who unknowingly broke their lives. They make them believe that they are protecting them from me, while they are the ones who make my children's lives hell.

They don't even let me contact my two daughters even if they are adults by now, and to lead a normal life with them; they cut off even communication through social media, making these children think that I am the one who abandoned them, and I am the one who harmed them.

Donati is still doing everything she can to keep my girls away from me. All this is to prevent my children from communicating with me and to keep the estrangement between the children and the mother lasting forever; this mother who sacrificed everything to get them back.

The psychologist, Valeria Donati, involved in Devils of 'Bassa Modenese area', or paedophiles of 'Bassa Modenese area'; the trial reopens:

"20 years later, Modena Court reopened investigations into the accusations that the psychologist Valeria Donati is instilled in the minds of children, in Mirandola County of Reggio Emilia, which turned out to be just that fake memory, took over children's minds after they were brainwashed, to admit in court that they were physically, psychologically, and sexually abused by their parents. As a result, some of the parents were wrongfully imprisoned, some died of choking, and others committed suicide. In

1998, Donati falsely accused more than 20 people of belonging to a sect of child molesters and Satanists which was alleged to have sexually, physically, and psychologically abused sixteen minors, in the house and across the cemeteries in the area. All children were removed from their families, and none had returned, it was she who made the children talking about dark rituals and demonic practices. The trial investigation proved that there were no satanic rituals, no murders were committed. It was also assumed that the methods of questioning the children led to the belief in these false memories. Investigative journalists, Pablo Trincia and Ravanelli met some children who are now adults and whom psychiatrist Donati has messed with when they were young, The journalists confirmed that: "We learned that suggestion can give birth to false, indelible memories over time, difficult to distinguish from real memories even after time has passed, sometimes they grow up believing that they were indeed the victims of sexual assault"

According to the data provided by the journalist Pablo Trincia, The Valeria Donati Child Aid Centre gets monthly, for each child followed, between 1,032 and 1,400 euros, and within 10 years it would have received the net amount of 2,209,400 euros from public money." It is evident that a real criminal organization has been set up, which has acted undisturbed for years, obtaining unfair profits on the skin of the people.

Such conduct should be punished in accordance with the provisions of Article 416 cp of the Italian Criminal Code for the crime of forming a criminal organization, as they acted through an organizational structure, such as to be able to have the necessary means for the realization of the criminal program or the prefiguration of an indeterminate series of crimes.

The offense in question is a permanent offense, which is committed when a partnership is born that is concretely capable of disturbing public order, or when the organizational structure takes on the characteristics such as this dangerousness.

The removal of all those children between February 1997 and November 1998 was the consequence of a series of blatant errors of evaluation by social services and investigative bodies, assisted by the psychologist Valeria Donati and her colleagues. They assumed that they discovered a group of paedophiles parents, which was proved false; accordingly, they destroyed entire families' members.

Several parents, who were accused wrongly, were sentenced to between four and thirteen years of imprisonment, others had also lost parental authority over their children, and others lost their lives; a mother, named Francesca, committed suicide after writing on a piece of paper: «I am innocent. I just want my daughter back». A father, Don Govoni, died of a heart attack in his lawyer's office, when he heard that he was sentenced.

One of these bad stories of invented accusations of paedophilia that destroyed so many lives in the lower Modena city arrives on television, it happened on Rai due during the program "I Fatti Tua", as follows:

"Michele Guardì's broadcast conducted by Giancarlo Magalli will tell what happened between Massa Finalese and San Felice. A surreal and crazy story in which entire families were ruined and still mourns those who died of a broken heart for the false accusations. The guest of the show is mother Lorenza Covezzi, the protagonist of this incredible drama.

The piece told the story of Lorena Morselli, a teacher asylum in Massa Finalese, in the province of Modena, who survived an endless judicial affair, in which she had been accused of abuses satanic rituals and sexual violence against her four children that she hadn't seen since they were little. Her story was creepy. At dawn on November 12, 1998, the police showed up at her house with her husband Delfin Covezzi, with an expulsion decree from the Juvenile Court of Bologna: an eight-year-old granddaughter followed by social services had them accused of being accomplices of a sect of depraved murderers that of the night he took the children of Massa to the cemeteries of the area, to rape them, sell them to a gang of paedophiles and make them participate in human sacrifices. A horror story I had never heard of, in one province made up of fields, secondary roads, farmhouses, trattorias and abandoned farmhouses, where apparently nothing ever happened. After listening carefully to the child, the psychologists and Mirandola's social workers had immediately alerted the authorities to also save the children of Lorena and Delfino Covezzi: Veronica was eleven years. Peter, nine years. Federico was seven years. Aurora was three years. They had been woken up altogether and were taken away within a few hours. To prevent her fifth child from being taken away too, she had in her womb, Lorena had run away to give birth abroad and she was there hidden with her baby in a small town in Province, the same place from which she answered the phone shortly after I had read the article and found her number.

The woman had a marked accent from the Lower Modena area, however, underpinned by French words and interlayers that she now used when she was lost in thought: oui, voilà, bon, donc, mais non!

attendez, alors, d'accord. Her story wasn't always straightforward. TO sometimes she looked more like the erratic, crooked flight of a butterfly.

Every so often, while she was telling the story, she remembered an episode, and at that point, she abandoned a memory to follow another, she opened parenthesis without closing any and she lost the thread. After that, giggling embarrassed, she resumed from a "well, donc, where were we left?" When the talk fell on her children, she did she moved, and the sentences ended in a strangled sob.

After leaving, the three older children confirmed the

testimony of the cousin, accusing Lorena of ferocious crimes: psychological violence, kidnapping, rape, and murder brutal in the cemeteries, where she and her husband had forced them to witness all kinds of crimes, forcing them to participate actively on more than one occasion. Once rescued by the social workers and the authorities, her children had rebuilt their lives in other ***families, and growing up they were convinced that the*** *parents had to pay with prison for all that bad. From that autumn morning in 1998, they hadn't wanted to anymore know anything about her.*
The Covezzi spouses had been sentenced to twelve years in primary judgment, and then acquitted in December 2014 after a long time the judicial procedure. But Delfino had never seen the end of the trial. He died of a heart attack the previous year.
I didn't know whether to believe her, Lorena's was a story full of gaps and dark sides. Because her children had told those things about her, I was confused, both as a journalist and as a father. Lorraine, she explained to me that it was the psychologists who had stuffed those stories in the heads of children, piloting them against their parents. But really women professionals could make such horrible tales and convince the little ones to repeat them? Why then? What if she had been?
Do you have a double soul? - Social services didn't just take my children, she said. - Between 1997 and 1998 in the two villages of Massa Finalise and Mirandola- had removed fourteen ... no, sorry ... fifteen indeed sixteen, all from families accused of the same things.''

Violence against minors of Donati and his colleagues

There are children whose lives have been ruined because they were torn from their parents, there are mothers and fathers who have never seen their children, grandmothers who have not seen their grandchildren grow up, and brothers who have been lost forever. It is enormous existential damage; one can speak of a violation of human rights.

With reference to the article that appeared on June 14, 2021, in "La Repubblica" entitled "Veleno", the" child zero" Davide, now 31 years old speaks: "They were all lies, I was forced to invent sexual abuse and satanic rites". Valeria resigned for fear of being killed because some of the children, victims of the "Bassa Modenese" (now they're adults) are threatening her with death, ***"I did my duty now I don't work anymore and I receive death threats***" Said Donati.

This psychologist oppressed my children, me and a load of families. Despite this, she said I did my duty; how can the destruction of entire families be a duty of psychology? What justice will be done when the unjust is the judge and the executioner himself?! In a court that is founded on injustice, the judge performs the task of the judge and the executioner at the same time.

Among the former children of the "Bassa Modenese" area - removed at a young age by their parents and investigated for sexual abuse of minors, and who today deny having been abused, is the girl **Marta** is now an adult. And in her interview with the journalist **Bruschi Viviana** said the following:

"WE PLAGUED TO INVENT ABUSE". MARTA: THIS IS HOW I WAS RIPPED FROM MUM"

Marta, why did you invent that you were abused?

"I was small at the time, I was eight years old. The psychologists of the social services of the Mirandola Ausl subjected us to real interrogations to frame the alleged paedophiles, including our parents. I am more than convinced that I was manipulated, of having told lies like so many other children ".

Of the sixteen taken from their families, four have retracted, including her. Will others do it?

"I hope so; the truth must have the victory over the lie. But you must have courage and above all have worked out what happened. It is not simple emotionally, it is a long process, and sometimes it takes a lifetime. I understand how many of us have not yet been able to take this step ".

What do you remember of that time away from home?

"That the psychologist Valeria Donati and other psychologists of the Ausl talked for hours with us children about black masses in the cemetery and about child pornography rites that Don Giorgio Govoni would have performed at the cemetery of Massa Finalese, in the "Bassa Modenese" area. We children were pressed to tell, and in the end, I think, we identified with the noir stories ".

Stories made by whom?

"From some child, one of whom he retracted months ago. The psychological pressure was such that we fell into the unconscious role of victims. After some time I understand that this story was invented at the table."

what is the reason?

"Don't ask me this, I don't have the answer. But I'm willing to do my duty as a citizen before the judge if the case is reopened because entire families have been destroyed, and so many people have died of pain. Those who have made a mistake must pay ".

Sonia, as she retracted, was the only one to shut herself up in silence during those years. Did she ask herself why?

"I think she was the strongest of us all, that we let ourselves be manipulated. I respect her a lot; I wanted to do the same thing. For years I had doubts, confusion, and slowly the truth emerged inside me. I had never been abused"

What do you remember of your childhood before you were taken away?

"It was my wonderful relationship with my mother. At that time she was cleaning the houses to support me and my brother, and I often accompanied her. I carried the satchel to do my homework. One day they took me away from home. The memory is vague: I know I was holding her so tightly that a policeman had to forcibly separate us."

Federica Anghinolfi

If we go back, we find a point of contact between my story, the kidnapping of my daughters by social workers in 2006 and the investigation of "angels and demons" that has led to the illegal adoption scandal. Anghinolfi, the former head of Social Services, who sold my children and wrote a report, accusing me of assaulting them, is actually one of the main characters in the investigation of the 'Bibbiano scandal'.

She is involved in many crimes against children and families. She is considered by the judiciary to be a central figure in the investigation into alleged illicit custody in this scandal. Federica Anghinolfi was fired from her job and no longer works as head of social services.

The disciplinary measure was taken by the office that has the service of disciplinary measures in agreement for the Reggio body and which belongs to the union of the Lower Romagna municipalities.

In the investigation papers, 50 of the 108 charges are mentioned about Anghinolfi including: false reports, misdirection, private violence, aggravated scam, procedural fraud, false ideological, psychological pressures, peculation of use, abuse of office, falsification of documents, minors abuse, very serious personal injuries, false accusations to parents to remove their children, Manipulating the words of the children in order to admit that they were subjected to abuse by their parents, which in fact did not happen, with hypotheses for various crimes against her.

The investigation was drafted by the prosecutor who coordinated the investigative activity of the Reggio Emilia Police. Anghinolfi, whose name still appears on the pages of major Italian newspapers, was reported that she gave many children in adoption for the benefit of gay couples to strengthen her relationship with them.

Anghinolfi has spoken on several occasions about her homosexuality and she is not ashamed to say it. She also confessed to abusing children saying: ***"What I did is what I did, I didn't do good things, and I was doing what the institution asked me to do."*** These and other statements made by Anghinolfi to journalist Carlotta Deiss in January 2020, In a report prepared for the Foro Dal Coro program, hosted by Mario Jordano, and it was broadcast on Riti Quattro on January 21, 2020.

To go back in July 2017, Anghinolfi was obsessed with accusing parents of sexual assault, upon questioning by Simona Piggy, Mayor of Bibbiano, Anghinolfi said:
"Violence can be found anywhere, I wake up at three, and I understand it is about work, too much child sexual abuse, too much violence in relationships, I wake up, as if I am looking for some relief". Her pinning the blame on parents was practically a confession of guilt, and an attempt to be above suspicion.

Despite misinformation, her matter was revealed in June 2019, in the scandal of Bibbiano, she was one of the main characters of the arrested gang, where children stolen from their biological parents and placed in a foster home or adoption in exchange for cash, children were victims of real brainwashing, with electrocution to confuse their memories until they believe that they were abused sexually by their parents.

Anghinolfi used to put pressure on social workers to write false reports: In the interview with a social worker named Cinzia Magnarelli who is one of those who was arrested in the scandal, confessed during the interrogation of the judge Luca Ramponi, by saying: ***"I was forging the reports to convince the Juvenile Court to take children away from families"*** The children are today at the centre of the investigation, considered victims of abuse. In her confession, Magnarelli spoke of pressure from her superiors and accused Federica Anghinolfi, the former director.

Anghinolfi entrusted a girl to a homosexual who abused the girl, and wiretapping revealing horrific details about how social workers would have managed to snatch children from their natural families and give them to delinquents and to the mentally ill people. It is the same cards that speak. And it all started like this:

"Holy shit, get off! Get off! I do not want you anymore! I don't want you anymore, come down! "This is one of the wiretaps of Daniela Bedogni and Fadia Basmajian, the homosexual couple involved in the custody scandal. "Do you think? Katia thinks that? Come on say it! Holy shit, go alone on foot "To scream is Daniela Bedogni. She yelled at the little girl that had taken in foster care with Fadia Bassmaji, and she does it because the little girl doesn't want to, indeed it would be better to say that she cannot, since the violence would never have occurred and she never spoke of abuses suffered in her natural family. Then, we always read in the papers, Daniela "throws the little girl out of the car in the pouring rain".

The Anghinolfi together with the senator of the PD, the mayor, and other monsters of the system, carry out a diabolical plan worthy of the worst criminals. The victims are children, they are fathers and mothers. Whole families destroyed only for the thirst for money and power by

perverse and sick minds. The weird thing is how these people are allowed to lead children's services.
Doesn't this in itself expose the Judicial Corruption and the gross negligence on the part of the Italian government?

For many years the judiciary has been hiring delinquent psychiatrists, psychologists, and social workers. It also contracts with private cooperatives, foster institutions, and foster families to collude in exploiting children. They unleash their utmost evil to satisfy their endless greed.

CHAPTER SEVEN

LUCRATIVE CORRUPT BUSINESS

Stealing more children to get more funding

Children have become a source of profit where business in human flesh and blood thrives. The Department of Child Protective Services requires many child victims for profit. To receive the adoption incentives or bonuses, local social services must have more children. They must have goods (children) to sell, and they must have plenty of them so the buyer can choose.

Adoption breeds corruption for several reasons. The demand for children to adopt keeps prices high, creating a fertile breeding ground for all sorts of illegal activity.

The annual turnover of 5 billion Italian euros for child trafficking is combined with very loose regulations and an almost complete lack of oversight, deception, child-stealing, and every transgression imaginable in order to obtain children to meet the demand.

As if infertile and same-sex couples seeking to adopt doesn't create enough demand, Child Protective Services intentionally over-report the number of orphans allegedly "languishing" in orphanages to tug at the heartstrings of buyers in order to increase profits. The line between legal, ethical adoptions and criminal activity is blurry at best.That in many foster institutes the fee exceeds 300-400 euros daily per minor/child. The honorary mentors of the juvenile courts operate in apparent professional contradiction, as the Chairman of the Inquiry Committee explains:

'These guides are psychologists, paediatricians, gynaecologists, psychiatrists, sociologists and social workers. They participate in the decisions to remove children from their families and at the same time have economic interests in the foster institutes, family homes, and cooperatives that welcome them."

The state gives financial incentives in the form of funding when the children are torn from their homes and placed in foster care. The foster family gets a daily wage exceeds 150 euro for each alternative care, and the secular or religious institutes receive an amount from 200 to 400 euros per day for each child: The BUSINESS that pretends HOSPITALITY.

Psychologists working in social services take up to 135 euros per session and always pretend that the child has medical needs and/or requires medication in order to get more funding.

Therefore, Foster children are often forced to take multiple psychotropic drugs. Psychologists and foster parents get extra "special needs" money for damaged kids, all paid by municipalities or public money. And if the child is adopted away from his/her family, more money is given.

The money goes to tens of thousands of criminal system employees and collateral professionals: Lawyers, court personnel, court investigators, evaluators, guardians, judges, counselors, therapists, junk psychologists, residential facilities, foster parents, adoptive parents, etc.

Social Workers and Juvenile Judges can always hide behind a confidentiality clause in order to protect their decisions and keep the funds flowing. The judicial part gets more funding by handling more cases, then, the sentences that are given too superficially are their daily bread.

The funding continues as long as the child is out of the home. Child Social Services run on a quota/bonus incentive system; the more children are removed from their parents; the more funding social services get. As a result, the total destruction tears apart children and families. Mandated by the local government, these programs are intended to provide a social safety net for our children and the elderly and a deterrent to domestic violence, but instead, they have become a mean by which the Child Protective Services extract great profits.

In exchange for providing the services, the local government reimburses them for the cost greatly more than the cost of that service. As such, these Child Protective Services find themselves sorely tempted to provide a service where one is not necessarily warranted (since reimbursements grow as the number of services rendered grows), Unfortunately, the provision of unnecessary services often ends up devastating those who are 'served'.

The system intends to break up and institutionalize whole families. It is an economic game that is played in broad daylight and in plain sight; without fear of the penalties of the local Supreme Court or the International Criminal Court.

The state funds the system, but the system is a corrupt business. Not in the best interest of children. The situation has become like big fish eating small fish and parents are not able to halt it from the ocean. Every passing day means more families and children are being held hostage and their lives destroyed.

There are NO financial resources and NO real drive to unite a family and help keep them together; that the incentive for social workers to return children to their parents quickly after taking them has disappeared. They are not following guidelines placing children with parents or relatives.

Corruption and end of parental authority

They are screening them out using different criteria with foster families or falsifying documents to entrap parents and remove children without due process or any true purpose other than to incriminate parents/family members and to ensure the family is unfit. Social workers are often times guilty of fraud. When a parent asks for assistance, they pretend to help and support. They mask their truth with politeness and gentleness; however, behind the doors, they plot how to undermine and damage families.

They fabricate evidence and seek to terminate parental rights. They use foxiness and tricks to abduct minors. Children are frequently and unjustly ripped from their parents and placed in foster care. These hardened criminals consider children a great feast and easy prey. They want to eat them all and devour them all!

The juvenile court gives unlimited power to social workers, demons of mankind, whose daily task is to strike terror into the hearts of children and remove them from their families even without any reason. Just for profit due to incentives from the state. The next step in the process is that social workers must appear in court and prove their cases. Judges, who share this enormous pie of money, allow them for fraudulent paperwork and perjury to occur relentlessly.

If the family hires a lawyer, the crimes have already begun with unlawful removal of the child, and even the best lawyer is incapable to do nothing, then the storm continues raging unabated. This system turns the war against children abuse to the war against children and parents.

The fraud is increased when the parents are poor and having attorneys appointed to them by the court system. In these cases, the appointed attorneys don't inform the parents of their rights or defending them against the social service institutions. The system is set up in a way that makes it more profitable, measures success, and the professionals are rewarded only if the child is removed and placed in foster care. The appointed attorneys get more pay the longer the process continues.

The judges get more funding by handling more cases. This also applies to foster care services, social workers and their psychologists. There is a huge bureaucracy made up of judges, court appointed Attorneys, Social Workers, Court Investigators, Therapists, Psychologists, Psychiatrists, Foster Parents, and on and on who are looking to the children in state care for their job security.

Social service institutions and the juvenile court system in which they work are secreted away, self-investigating, and exist under laws and limitations of criminal prosecution that violate the laws and statutes of the nation. They pay themselves off and can act without limit. This imbalance of funding is creating corruption. The monopoly strategy of funding obtained from deceptive social services that set up to help families, is now devastating families across Italy.

They are not rewarded for preserving rights of the child and the parent or assisting families and returning the child to them when it is appropriate. This mafia funded by the people of the nation, smiles and reassures you just as the fangs of a lion are prominent– ''When you see the lion's fangs sticking out, don't think the lion is smiling''.

We all know that social service is established for good intentions of ''protecting'' children and concerning with individuals and families to enhance social performance and general well-being. It is the way in which people perform their social roles and the structural institutions that are provided to support them.

However, social services are wrapped into other institutions as an instrument of punishment. Their mission has been devalued to the point of being shrouded in mystery and intrigue between them and families. The tension is reaching its maximum since they have used various harmful and abusive means to pursue their interests at the expense of the vulnerable, mistreating the innocent, and causing long-lasting suffering.

Social workers, in fact, are helpers of lucrative deals. They are trained to manage evil deeds, mix protection papers with greedy papers, and mix suspicious with certainty. Consequently, parents lose the ability to distinguish between social services and criminal gangs, between truth and falsehood, and between right and wrong. Social service primary duty is no longer giving priority to the public interest over the private interest within the framework of respect for the law. It has become adult centered to the detriment of children.

No longer is judgment based on what the child needs, which the child wants to be with, or what is really best for the whole family; it is some adult or bureaucrat who makes the decisions, based often on just hearsay without ever consulting a family member.

There are a few good people in these institutions, but I am afraid that they might be intimidated and forced into silence. Few of the so-called "honourable" men and women still fight against this corrupt system to protect the rights of innocent child victims, and others are targeted by the regime itself to render them powerless, because they are considered an obstacle to achieving personal and economic interests above all.

Among the fighters of corrupt child protection system is the former juvenile judge Francesco Morcavallo who refused to apply the injustice and human rights violations committed by his colleagues at the juvenile court in Bologna city. It is the court where Judge Francesca Salvatore had kidnapped and sold my children.

Morcavallo was interviewed on 'Panorama' TV program. He exposed the dangerous tactics and overt corruption that had witnessed as a judge in the juvenile court.

The interview was published on "**il Desk quotidiano independenti,**" by the journalist Maurizio Tortorella on July 21, 2019, as follows: *"He appears to be a thoughtful and perhaps sad man, Francesco Morcavallo. If so, then the reason is defeat. Because, despite a battle that lasted nearly four years, he was unable to move an inch of what he considers a 'harmful mechanism' and at the same time* *the "most horrible Italian business": the very easy foster care of tens of thousands of children in a relentless machine of the judiciary system. From September 2009 to May 2013, as a judge at the juvenile court in Bologna, Morcavallo witnessed many of those dramatic cases that begin with the abduction of children and end up with what he calls "incarceration" (often for years) in foster care institutes and foster family homes run by social services. As a judge, Morcavallo also fought a culture war against what he saw around him. He tried to correct wrong behaviour. He tried to confront an incredibly conflict of interest. He also reported the abuses and gross violations committed by his colleagues. He was in turn hit by complaints, and came out unharmed, but then he didn't make it and changed his path''*

''Doctor Morcavallo, how many children have been removed each year by the juvenile court, like the one in Bologna, 'on average'? Are there tens, hundreds?

''There are thousands. But the truth is that no one really knows how many there are, anywhere in Italy. The most recent study, perhaps even the only one on the subject, is from 2010: The Ministry of Labour and Social Policy calculated that as of December 31 of that year the children and young people taken away from their families were a total of 39,698. In Emilia alone there were 3,599. But the ministerial statistics are much inferior to the truth; I believe that a realistic number exceeds 50,000 cases. And that abandonment prevails.''

Abandonment?

''When I arrived in Bologna in 2009, there were about 25,000 open proceedings, loads of them were for too many years. I found a file that dates back to 1979: paradoxically, it referred to a peer of mine, evidently still entrusted to social services as a child and then 'followed' up to the age of majority, without interruption. The file was still there, no one had ever closed it''

And what else did you find at the Bologna Court?

''We, magistrates, were seven, including the president Maurizio Millo. Then there were 28-30 honorary judges: psychologists, doctors, sociologists, social workers.''

How had the work been done?

''The judicial panels, as required by law, should have been made up of two magistrates and two honorary judges: chosen automatically, with neutral, pre-established logic. Instead, there was obvious confusion. The result was that the colleges were made up of 'a variable geometry'. With only one goal.''

That is?

''A dozen judges met in the courtroom and dealt with the various cases; from time to time the four 'decision makers' who would then have had to sign the ordinance were chosen by co-optation, exclusively on the basis of the opinions expressed. In short, everything was organized in such a way as to make the setting of social services prevail, always and inevitably in favour of the removal of the minor.''

And what did you do?

''I immediately began to clash with many colleagues and especially with President Millo. Our approaches were too different: I have always been convinced that the interest of the minor must prevail, and that his remaining in the family wherever possible coincides with this interest. It is the 'least invasive' line, the same one followed by the Constitutional Court and the European Court of Human Rights.''

Did the other judges have different ideas from yours?

''Yup. They were for the removal, almost always. Only an elderly colleague opposed the system as I did: Guido Stanzani. He had been a magistrate since 1970, an honest

and serious man. And even some honorary judges shared our commitment: in particular the psychologist Mauro Imparato.''

What was going on? How did the proceedings begin?

''In the vast majority of cases it was a question of removing children from families for economic reasons or because the parents were considered "incompetent".''

What does "incompetent" mean?

''Just getting a report from social workers; just a psychologist pretends parents are 'too care on themselves. In many cases, it is evident, these are events served for certain purposes, which start from conflicting separations. The problem is that all court proceedings are final.''

Why?

''Because these are formally 'provisional' measures. Removal from the family, for example, is by its nature a provisional act. Thus, even if it lasts for years, by law it cannot be the subject of an appeal request. In short, we cannot oppose it; not even the best lawyer can do anything about it.''

Among the causes of child removal, however, there are also reports of sexual abuse in the family. In those cases, is it not good to use every possible caution?

''Where it was about alleged violence, a share anyway less than 5 percent, in Bologna I saw that many cases were opened irritably due to anonymous letters. It was the classic neighbour who wrote beware; in that house they molest their children. There was no proof. But social services reported, and the court removed. It is arbitrary and serious abuse because an anonymous report should be discarded. Instead, it was enough to justify the custody. Moreover, if you think that many honorary judges were and are in conflict of interest, there is some

reason to understand why.''
What do you mean?

''Who are the honorary judges? They are psychologists, sociologists, doctors, social workers. They have often founded institutes. And sometimes even the same foster homes that take care of children stolen from families, and precisely for an ordinance in which they participated.''
Possible?

''In Bologna, I found an honorary judge at the hearing who was there, at the same time, also as 'guardian' of the minor on whose foster care we had to judge.''
But are honorary judges paid?

''Yup, so much for the audience, so much for each act. I insist some hold 20-30 hearings a week and collect the court fees, but in the meantime, they also work for institutes, cooperatives that welcome minors. It is an obscene and rich business, because almost always children and young people are entrusted to the foster institutes for months, often for years. And the fees are sometimes high: there are municipalities and local health companies that pay from 200 to over 400 euros per day. Let's say that the business is powered by those who have every interest in it growing.''
It is a serious complaint. Is the phenomenon so widespread? Is it possible that everyone is interested, the honorary judges? That all the foster institutes only look to business?

''No, of course. Even, in this sector there is the bad and there is the good, indeed the excellent. Obviously, there are those who work selflessly. But the phenomenon is fed in the same way for everyone. The courts of minors do not choose where to place minors taken from families, but it happens that choice is up to the social services. However, the exponential growth of foster care and fees

is the same for the good as for the bad. And there are those who gain from it.''
Are there good or bad institutes for you?

''I do not know. In my view, good are those that promote contact between children and families. There are a few. I know 2 or 3 of them.''
But, sorry: who appoints honorary judges?

''The concerned person directly presents the application, the juvenile court approves it, the Higher Council of the Judiciary ratifies it.''
And no one reports conflicts of interest? Nobody blocks them.

''The presidents of juvenile courts should do so by law. The CSM could do it. But nothing ever happens. The Finally Free association, to which I have joined, is among the few that have decided to investigate and is doing it on a large scale. Hundreds of honorary judges have been identified so far in a clear conflict of interest. We will report them. We'll see if anyone will follow us.''
How much is what you call "obscene business" worth?

''Hard to say, nobody checks. In Italy there is not even a register of custody, as happens in almost all Western countries.
You assume an estimate.

''There are at least 50,000 minors in custody: I believe they cost 1.5 billion a year, maybe more.''
Let's go back to Bologna. In January 2011 a serious event happened: a new-born died in Piazza Grande. It was there that the conflict between you and the president of the juvenile court broke out. How did it go?

''The mother had given birth to twins ten days earlier.

One of the two died from being exposed to the cold. What happened? In reality, the family, declared indigent, had two other older children, both entrusted to social services. The case landed on my desk. I investigated and became convinced that this death was due to desperation. The parents had a home, contrary to what the newspapers had written, but they ran away because they were terrified by the prospect that the two babies would also be taken away from them.''

And what happened at that point?

''President Millo called me. He said: let's call the college immediately and suspend parental authority. I replied: let's see, first, what the college decides. Millo took the procedure to himself, an act not foreseen by any norm, then proceeding, an act not foreseen by any norm, so I presented a complaint to the CSM, denouncing all the anomalies I had seen. And a month later Stanzani made another exposition. They were followed by one of Imparato and one of the Emilian family lawyers.''

Was it then that the conflict broke out?

''Yup. I was reached by a disciplinary precautionary measure from the CSM. I was accused of having said that the Juvenile Court of Bologna was administering a justice more suited to North Korea, of having denigrated President Millo. I was transferred to Modena as a labour judge. Stanzani was also transferred, while Imparato was marginalized. In December 2011, however, the United Sections Supreme Court annulled that decision by harshly criticizing the CSM because it had not listened to my reasons, nor had it followed up on my complaints.''

So, you went back to Bologna?

''Yup. But due to the delays of the CSM, also illegitimate, the return took place only on 18 September 2012. In the meantime, Millo had left, but not much had changed. I was put to deal with the older cases: pending issues

dating back to 2009. I was excluded from any new adoptability procedure. I understood then why a magistrate of the Attorney General of the Cassation a few months earlier had suggested that I had to give up, that I was giving too much trouble to people who could have made me desist by powerful means."

Are you saying you were threatened?

"Let's put it this way: I was warmly invited not to bother any more. I realized that it was all in vain, that the wall did not fall. Meanwhile, in March, Stanzani had died. I decided to leave the judiciary."

And now?

"Now I'm a lawyer. But I work from outside to make things change. I speak at conferences, write, and ask indiscreet questions."

What are you asking?

"For example, that the prosecutors in the juvenile courts go to check the foster care institutes: they never do it, but it is a real shame because they would certainly find many surprises. I also ask that the National Childhood Supervisor show more courage, that he uses the skills he mistakenly believes he does not have, that he investigates. Someone will have to do it. It is an all-Italian scandal: it must be uncovered."

As we notice from the testimony of the juvenile judge who was fired for opposing the intolerable injustice, it is a shocking reality that spreads all over the country.

The spreading of fraud and arbitrary decisions by putting minors' lives in danger and trampling their rights underfoot show the government's contempt for the Italian justice system.

Thus, Juvenile Court is no longer open to 'justice' or bolster the nation's 'security'. It is based on the wrong principle of child trafficking for quick profit and do not deliver justice.

The government indifference threatens greater corrosion of the rights of the children and families in Italy, in the name of "Child Protection." It provides cover for judges' mistakes and shields judges' wrongdoing from public and judicial scrutiny under conditions that are fair and just.

It is the age of obscurity and ambiguity. The age of the deadliest virus; it is a virus of money slavery at the expense of the innocent. Judges easily make decisions to remove children, social workers kidnap these children and drown in a sea of lies, and psychologists forge documents and distort children's minds. And no one is held accountable for their actions!

CHAPTER EIGHT

KIDNAPPING CHILDREN AND DECEIVING PARENTS

Hiding behind the "child protection" slogan to exploit it

Kidnapping, fraud, coercion, and perjury occur openly and every day. Social workers and juvenile judges stab, shatter children, and turn them into commodities. Since the task is filthy, it must be done by people who have the qualities of filth, greed, and coveting to profit from the weak. They intend to tear minors to shreds, slaughter them as sheep, and put them up for auction. It is incredible, horrible, but TRUE!

Child Protective Services are over time degraded and dehumanised, a trend most apparent under the Italian power. Their holders cheat and disappoint parents by committing the most horrific forms of crime. Children are detained in foster institutions, religious institutions, cooperatives, foster family homes, and ended up in adoption for an agreed price. Social workers advertise children online and in "adoption markets" to find homes for thousands of forcibly removed children.

Child Protective Services have become a "protected monster empire" built on separating families, robbing and selling children. Most cases that involve the removal of children from their homes are shifted to become ''removal without any cause.'' It is ineffective policies where corruption runs wild, leaving citizens with no laws to protect them.

Common tactics of child confiscation system are based on several issues such as poverty, parental incompetence, domestic violence, divorce, disability, the necessity of medical support, unspecified medical conditions, autism, to name a few, under the guise of an "emergency protection order" to extract children. Not only do social workers act upon these conditions, whether the child or the parent has them. They willfully, perversely distort them as means to acquire the intended commodity–children. And if one of these conditions doesn't already exist, social workers make false accusations against parents to justify taking away the children.

Intimidation along with vindictive or punitive action against parents who dare attempt to question the process or to stand up for their family's rights is just part of the process. Loving parents are often accused of abusing their children, so they unfairly face imprisonment. This tyrannical government overwhelms the weak in society terribly.

Thousands of children look like dead corpses; their minds, bodies and souls imprisoned together in an environment where morals are shaken, collapsed, and respectively extinguish all the candles of innocence and joy. Children are completely devoured by predators. The prey is not just a loss for humans; it is an asset for Child Protective Services and Juvenile Courts that hide behind the totally baseless slogan of "child protection." These hardened criminals regard children as a huge feast and easy prey. They want to eat them all and devour them all mercilessly!!

There is no safeguarding or protection for the welfare of the child, but deception, abuse, brainwashing and trafficking. It's a terrible game played by the LEGAL MAFIA that is funded by the government. They horribly run BIG BUSINESS through illegal foster care and adoption, and they rake in billions of euros each year.

Hundreds of thousands of children/young people are stolen from their families and placed in foster institutions and foster family homes. Worse still, this custody is ordered by the juvenile court for an indefinite period, thereby preventing the children from returning to their birth parents. So, this illegal custody turns into a disguised adoption process that hides economic interests.

The government does not protect the public from this domestic terrorism. Children's interests are not their top priority. The government holders are manipulative, deaf, and disingenuous! Those who do not wish to please the public and do not realize the need to respond, and those who continue to follow the same rhetoric and policies despite the suffering of the public.

All family rights are violated

The fact that all due process, constitutional and human rights are violated and manipulated by bad court judges, social services departments, as well as psychologists, psychiatrists, and court-appointed attorneys who don't work for clients but help incriminate the parents. The court-appointed attorneys have an extreme interest too, conspiring with social workers who falsify documents and lie in a court setting.

The story of child trafficking is organised by social workers and their psychologists, sanctioned by juvenile courts, and approved by politicians who have tried to keep it secret since the 1970s. This does not mean that there are no children who need to be kept out of miserable situations and need protection. This report concerns children and parents who have been caught in "legal abduction," and those who bear the consequences of unresolved suffering.

Child Protective Services nationwide have become corrupt. The entire system is broken almost beyond repair. The system cannot be trusted because it does not serve the people. It ruins families and children simply because it has the power to do so. Children are taken in the middle of the night, out of schools, out of homes and new-born babies removed from their mothers' arms out of hospital and renamed. The result is a loss of identity with no names to connect those victims to their history or heritage.

If the children's lives are improved by taking them away from their homes, there may be a greater need for Child Social Services. But today not all children are always safer. The child is much more likely to be sexually abused and even die when in foster/institutional care. Too many cases of tolerated paedophilia and violence against minors are gradually emerging even in environments that are considered to be the most accredited guardians of childhood.

Juvenile Judges indirectly encourage "child abuse'' by entrusting minors to homosexual, sex shops, and people with serious mental health conditions who emotionally, sexually, and physically abuse the children; a scandal of Northern Italy has recently proved that.

Children are exhausted from complaining because they consider adults totally unable to understand and act in their favour. Grieving parents still weep and cry out for fairness and justice. Unfortunately, their cries are ignored by the Italian state. Their suffering is overwhelming; most of them do not know where their children are, and have not seen them for a long time.

CHAPTER NINE

TRAFFICKING AND TERRIBLE CHILD ABUSE

Social workers pretend that children are removed from their homes because of horrible abuse and are sent to loving foster homes where they will thrive. But far too often that is just not true. Most of the abuses occur in foster families and foster institutions, headed by psychologists and social services, where children are miserable and exploited.

Our Children are being placed with strangers and sold like cattle into slavery and sex trade, and unfit homes where they are being abused, starved, beaten, tortured, and even murdered. Children are seven times more likely to be harmed in foster/adoption care than they ever would have been with their own families.

Children's lives are at stake while in the care of government funded social services, such as rape, sexual abuse, physical abuse, mental abuse, and neglect. Statistics show our children are being terribly abused while in government placements outside of the parental home. I am explaining some sorts of abuse that our children suffer, and which can carry a substantial risk of causing physical and emotional harm;

Overmedication in foster care

My heart is heavy as I write these words because I have

already known about my children, who have been harmed by drugs after becoming foster children. The tragedy is that the harm is still befalling many precious and innocent children.

Thousands of foster kids appear to be on powerful psychotropic or mind-altering drugs. Many of them are barely in kindergarten. Child Protective Services and their staff doctors are even defrauding the medication programs by prescribing medication that a child doesn't need or by overwhelmed it for each kidnapped child.

For instance, they remove a child who is perfectly happy and healthy, have him diagnosed with special need conditions and disorders, medicate him with psychotropic drugs he does not need because if the child has medical needs or requires medication, more funding is available.

In addition to that, children from troubled homes often have anger and aggression issues, and it is often prescribed drugs to "contain" their behaviours so they won't get bounced from foster home and foster institute.

The Italian Citizens' Human Rights Committee, which still focus on the tragedy of children harmed by the system that pretends to protect them, unfold some terrible news about over-medication of foster children.

This committee has described the situation of some children who exposed to medication overdose abuse; they have seemed like completely different and have been suffering from terrifying hallucinations and nightmares.

According to this committee: Not enough resources are being directed to caring for these children and giving them the therapies and the intensive treatment; This is what they need, not drugs. That's a lot of time, that's a lot of people to do that – therapists, counselors, and doctors -- and that of course all costs money.

States are opting to just make children undergo extensive intake of drugs instead.

Giving regular medication to foster children will qualify them as "special needs" that means more federal money is available, and this is itself a tragedy. These children do not need psychoactive substances -- they need the best human, caring services that our society can provide. The drugs may make them temporarily more docile, but by disrupting and suppressing normal brain function and development, they add new stressors to their lives and prevent them from adapting and growing as best as possible.

Brainwashing minors and hidden dark abuses

Minors are subjected to a severe form of brainwashing in misjudged psychology. It's the absurd danger of the situation. As therapists ruined my daughters' lives, I've learned things that are practiced by most manipulative and evil people out there to achieve terrible things; to get minors to believe things that are not true, and actions that have never happened. They actively break down identities and replace them with false beliefs that serve their criminal organization target.

Children are convinced of their parents' complete disinterest in their suffering. They are plagiarized to believe that they have been saved from family members who cared little or nothing about them. While Mum and Dad are screaming for justice from their homes, powerless before the decisions of the social services and the juvenile court and trapped in false accusations that only time can prove them wrong.

These dangerous criminals use different methods to distort the image of parents in the eyes of these children. The first tactic to be used in brainwashing minors, by social workers and their psychologists is typically to isolate the victim away from their family and relatives. Children are also kept out of sight from anything that connects them with their relationships to the past. The reason for doing this is so that the victim only has the manipulator to talk to, who can shape him as he wants and can implant in his brain what he likes, and there is no third party coming in and questioning what's going on.

At psychotherapy sittings during which children are also given electroshock therapy to alter their memories. False memories of sexual abuse can be generated through coercion and electrical impulses. The therapists also use dangerous methods of child interrogation. They ask children direct, repeated questions.

It is realized that these methods are very likely to create disclosures of events that never happened. From this source, many dozens of innocent adults have been charged with performing ritual abuse, sexual abuse, etc. Hundreds of adults have been imprisoned for crimes that never happened. Thousands of children have grown up with false memories of the most horrendous forms of neglect, maltreatment, and abuse that never occurred.

The psychologists and psychiatrists, who work for social services, often disguise themselves as evil characters from fairy tales to represent the parents so that children will be affected by the image they are taught about their parents, and then will describe them negatively in trials.

As they are approaching the judicial interviews, they have been really "brainwashed." The electrical impulses are passed off as "memory machines" and instead will "alter the state of memory in the vicinity of the judicial interviews."

Many children, after having 'The electrical impulses' that generate false records into children's minds, experience more long-lasting or permanent memory loss; including losing personal memories of forgetting information they need to continue in their school or make sense of their personal relationships.

Definitely, when minors form an impression of their parents as they are continuously brainwashed by psychiatrists, psychologists, social workers, and educators; those repetitive negative words are always at the forefront of their brains.

Sexual abuse in foster care

Social service professionals who run the child protection fraud industry join the ranks of people who expose children to sexual exploitation everywhere and by any means. These criminally intentioned find lucrative means to obtain their victims through an already corrupted system. And will soon see greater streams of children brought to foster homes.

Bibbiano scandal is just a tip of an iceberg that has explored horrifying abuses that victims suffer including sex trafficking, where there were confirmed cases of rape and sexual violence in foster families and in foster institutions; while many foster parents have been accused of sexually abusing the children that they paid money for.

Children who are entrusted to social workers and nuns are sold to paedophiles, sex shops, gays, people with severe mental health conditions, and people whose children committed suicide. Children end up in much worse situations than they started with.

Child abusers are routinely being approved as foster parents, which allow child sex trafficking to continue in Italy. More of this practice of approving sex offenders and paedophiles to become foster parents, to meet the demand of the lucrative child sex trafficking business.

These forms of abuse may last a lifetime and can include brain damage and hearing and vision loss, resulting in disability. They can cause the child to lose confidence and develop an inferiority complex. According to the Centres for Disease Control and Prevention, physical and sexual abuse can cause lifelong psychological, physical, behavioural, and economic problems.

Victims will also most likely struggle with poor physical and mental health as a result. Aside from observable signs of physical damage, the effects of this abuse might manifest as depression, anxiety, or high-risk behaviours such as casual sex, self-harm, crime, chemical dependency, and other unhealthy, dangerous behaviours

The effects of child sexual abuse usually include low self-esteem, a feeling of worthlessness, a lack of trust in adults, and an abnormal or distorted view of sex. The effects can be so strong that the child may even become suicidal. Children who have suffered from sexual abuse are also at an increased risk of future abuse and may become child abusers themselves.

Children who develop depression and anxiety due to their abusive past often turn to dangerous behaviours to cope with their emotional and psychological scars.

Misjudged psychology in foster care

"Incredible" stories which have nothing incredible, just the fact that they can really happen in every Italian city. They all have a common thread that unites them like beads of a necklace: Psychiatry that makes itself Justice, and the Justice adopting Psychiatry. Big stuff, huh! And for this, even if not only for this reason, that they are called "Crazy cases". "Psycho-judicial cases?" Maybe. More simply, cases.

Violence, bullying, harassment, abuse, usurpations, and provocations, in a word, suffering without end for those who remain entangled inside and cannot receive who could help them - THE LAW! - The help of that outstretched hand that the Constitution described so well.

In Italy, through evaluations - by their very nature subjective and questionable - psychiatrists, psychologists, consultants, and social workers, who are indoctrinated on the biological model of the mind and unable to use common sense and humanity, and through subjective and questionable assessments may induce the juvenile court to take drastic and dramatic measures, removing the children from the family, placing them in tutelary communities for minors, then putting them under investigation, analysis and so on.

''This is yet another demonstration that the encounter between psychology/psychiatry and justice can cause unspeakable damage, as in the case of the child who forced to see his alleged executioner on the basis of abstract psychological theories. It is our duty to bring justice back to the correct tracks!'' said Silvio De Fanti, Vice President of the Citizens' Committee for Human Rights.

"In the recent conference in Milan 'Psychiatry and distortion of justice', organized by CCHR and by the Italian section of LIDU - International League for Human Rights, in fact, Professor Morris Ghezzi, full professor of Philosophy and Sociology of the Right to University of Milan, argued that the judge is no longer expert of experts, who listens to the opinions of the experts but then reserves the right to make an independent assessment - but has transferred the function of social control to medicine, and to psychiatry in particular."

CHAPTER TEN

CHILD PROTECTIVE SERVICES SCANDAL

I have always had questions about a backward system that throws the honourable into the gutter, humiliates the dearest, and turns the war against child abuse into a war against children. But I was shocked and appalled when I realized how much the children had been suffering under horrific conditions, inflicting severe physical and psychological harm on them.

Scandal "Angels and Demons" in Bibbiano

Although they are children and share childhood traits: Innate humour, delicate feelings, purity of heart, and innocent smile; they differ from their peers. Their liberty is imprisoned, and their innocence is killed.

They are kidnapped, raped, brainwashed, and sold. This brings back memories of the gangsters portrayed in the movies; however, this is in fact the scandal of the Italian government institutions established for the welfare and protection of families and children. This is the biggest scandal of the child protection system, and the biggest cover-up the bitter result of state collusion, which ultimately forced a commission of investigation.

The scandal's code-name "**Angels and Demons** has sparked in Bibbiano, province of Reggio Emilia city, and has been reported by several national and international media including 'INDEPENDENT' the British Newspaper, that has apprised the following:

<u>Alessio Perrone, Friday 28th June 2019</u>

''Mayor, doctors and social workers arrested in scheme to brainwash children into believing they had been abused and sell them Network fabricated evidence and made children believe they had been abused in adoption scheme worth hundreds of thousands of euros: Italian police have arrested 18 people, including a mayor, social workers and psychologists for allegedly "brainwashing" children into believing their parents had abused them, in a scheme to take them away from their families and sell them to foster parents. Authorities in the central Italian city of Reggio Emilia revealed how a network of caregivers allegedly used hours of psychotherapy sessions and electroshocks to convince children their parents had sexually abused them and "alter their memory ahead of the trials", Italy's Ansa news agency reports. They then allegedly sold the children on to friends and acquaintances in a scheme worth hundreds of thousands of euros. The investigations, codenamed "Angels and Demons", started in the summer of 2018 after police received a series of reports of wrongdoing that initially proved false. The 18 arrested include Andrea Carletti, mayor of Bibbiano, a town of about 10,000 near Reggio Emilia, as well as politicians, doctors, social workers and psychologists. The network initially fabricated false reports to take children away from disadvantaged families. Then they proceeded to convince the children that they had indeed been abused. In an episode reported by Italian newspaper 'La Repubblica', a girl said she couldn't remember why she couldn't see her father anymore.

"But don't you remember you said you didn't want to see him? I remember this," a psychologist told her.

"I didn't say that" the girl replied.

"Yes, you said you didn't want to see him because you were afraid that he would hurt you..." the psychologist quoted as insisting. "That he might seek vengeance... or take you away. Do you remember the fear you felt? Do you remember now?"The child allegedly said she didn't remember and that she cried because she missed her father.

To brainwash the children and deceive authorities, the network is also accused of using small electroshocks that they called the "little memory machine" while with children.

Their other methods allegedly included forging childlike drawings to add fake sexual details, falsely describing their parents' homes as derelict, and enacting plays in which social workers playing the children's parents disguised as monsters trying to harm them.

Speaking while at the G20 summit in Osaka, Japan, Italian Prime Minister Giuseppe Conte said: "These accusations, if confirmed, are frightening and shocking."

Investigators also believe that social workers never gave the children dozens of presents and letters sent by their natural parents.

Authorities said the scheme tried to "pass off as a model welfare system for abused minors what was in reality an illegal business to the children's detriment".

The children's foster parents included sex shop owners, people with psychological disorders and parents whose children had taken their lives. Italian media report that two of the children have been sexually abused after being assigned to the foster parents.

Along with the 18 arrested, dozens of others are under investigation.

The group is accused of a long series of crimes including abusing minors, grave injuries, and abuse of power, embezzlement, judicial fraud and fabricating evidence. Italian media report that dozens of people are under investigation."

The former director of social services, Federica Anghinolfi, who was implicated in this scandal, was the one who deprived me of my daughters and sold them. She used to team up with other demonic figures that used other terrifying methods to destroy families, among these figures is the psychologist Valeria Donati who adopted one of my daughters after brainwashing them. This psychologist is the heroine of the crimes of the "Diabolic Panic" case, which returns to court after two decades, (See the shocking details in Chapter eight)

In the scandal 'Angels and Demons'– Investors began investigating, and what came out was a civil and political earthquake. The social workers wanted to make money on the fostering of minors and, to do so; they manipulated the minds of the children and created drawings of their own that could suggest the suffering of these children.

Psychologists make money through therapy sessions. And this excessive power that social services have acquired over the years has led to stories like this. Stories that you think you can only see in a horror movie and that instead, in the most absurd way possible, have come to reality, translating a mere round of money and power into the unhappiness of many children and their families.

Hundreds of thousands of euros were involved, Italian media reported. The attorney general 'Valentina Salvi', who is dealing with the case of this scandal, in Reggio Emilia tribunal, confirmed that:

''The lives of thousands of children are at stake. Five hundred thousand to be exact'' The Italian organization CDDU have commented on the number that: *''In foster care institutions, the figure may seem frightening, but it is the number of children followed by social services that fund this system, fueled by psychiatric diagnoses, and made up of local services, home education cooperatives, and office technical consultants. There is an estimated turnover of around 5 billion (billions not millions) of euros, which are paid for by the municipalities, or with public money''*

The probe codenamed ''Angels and Demons'' revealed a scheme to pass off as a model welfare system for abused minors what was in reality an illegal business to the children's detriment. According to investigators, the aim of the arrested group was to take children away from families in difficult social situations and give them in exchange for money to other parents, including those who suffer from mental illnesses or whose children have committed suicide.

Despite the 'Angel and Demons' scandal that shook Italy, and despite the media echo that accompanied it, it has now been forgotten. The trial linked to this scandal is still being postponed. In the hearing of 11 March 2021, and on the lengthening of the times, **judge 'Dario De Luca' allowed himself a joke by saying: "I have no intention of continuing this process until 2045''**.

Undisputedly, delaying the achievement of justice is an injustice itself. The time has come for justice to be served! Justice is not just sweet talk and false promises; it is serious work and a step forward to deter criminals. Justice demands full restoration of the rights of the oppressed, defense of the weak, and impartiality in trials of friends and acquaintances.

Scandal of the 'Serinper' foster care home

They call it foster care, but too often it is a robbery. The case of children illegally stolen from their families in this scandal is probably the tip of the iceberg. A real turnover emerges that enriches non-profit associations, cooperatives, sociologists, social workers, psychologists, and "honorary judges". But you know this happens all the time!

The scandal, however, hasn't stopped. In Massa Carrara city; politics, psychiatrists, and Juvenile Judges increased the earnings on children's skin. The December 2020 investigation brought 8 public figures to jail. The managers of the 'Serinper community' (Marina di Massa) were also accused, which, according to the mothers, treated parents and children in the worst way, for example by preventing mothers from breastfeeding their children for several days..

To date, the two communities, 'Serinper and Casa Famiglia Sorrisa', under investigation and accused of ill-treatment, continue to host minors and parents. In one evening, the parents were given a calming herbal tea that, in reality, contained anxiolytics and medicines. In the morning they woke up inexplicably tired and then the educators told them that they were probably no longer able to play the role of parents.

The testimonies of the mothers are chilling. One of them says that as a threat, social workers often carried a blank sheet on which they asked the mother to write a waiver of the child. One of them committed suicide when her two daughters had been taken away from her. Another mother says that she witnessed the death of a child at the hands of an educator.

Horrendous as it sounds, it's true: child abuse has become a business – and industry of sorts – that actually pays funds to legally abduct your children and put them up for adoption!

The details that make these scandals even more egregious, especially if you think about the years gone by and the alleged unspeakable suffering of children, victims of violence who have been subjected to traumas so complex that may affect them for the rest of their lives.

The failure of the local authority to act on reports of abuse over the ages, and the failure to address this abuse, is due to the fact that the state does not take into account the children's welfare or what is best for them.

Your fear of the criminal organization is real

I am convinced that parents and families should be warned of the danger. Parents need to be aware of methods to protect themselves and their children from wild social services attack. Their uncontrolled power is illegal.

These individuals all demonstrate the barbarism of conflict and savagery, where extremely violent and cruel behaviours take place, and in which other people are not respected and recoil with horror. The horror of kidnapping, the horror of dumbing, and the horror of paedophilia that disturbs the innocence and future of children.Their avarice has driven them to commit crimes.

They are completely submitted to the primitive natural instincts of the human soul. They cannot control their instincts and upgrade their behaviour. They can't get over their instincts. They cannot channel their energy into more refined and polite patterns of behaviour. Those savages who are given the reins are not worthy of it because they are unqualified and untrustworthy.

They commit heinous crimes against children. They play with people's lives, thousands of victims who do not have the slightest relationship with any issue. They use coercion on parents and several barbaric attacks, where victims are dehumanized and not looked as a human being, only as enemies to be crushed. The obsession of obtaining more money leads them to become money hungry; their greed is never satisfied, and their journey carries them through an unfortunate trail to betrayal.

Despite that, their lack of human morality makes them boast of transgressing the law or of being able to extract privileges through violence and crimes of child abduction and rape, where the concept of magnanimity and strength is considered one of the most distorted concepts.

The stubbornness of their aggression and the decline of their motives of domination, deviance, corruption, villains, slavery to money and treachery of the children of the country, make things go from bad to worse there, making your children missing and among the dead.

No benevolence, no goodness inside those who eat the children of their country!

Are you a nation that accepts the cruelty of ripping children from their parents' arms and exploiting them? Or are you a nation that values families, and works to keep them together? Are your courts ruled by fair judges? Or are your courts abused by the real criminals?

CHAPTER ELEVEN

THE LAW IS NOT EQUAL FOR EVERYONE

Crimes without punishment

Courts are marred by widespread corruption. Irresponsibility, partiality, and unfairness occur in courtrooms publicly. Courts' documents show the fact that civil rights are violated, and all human rights are violated. The behaviour of the legal criminal organization that claim the protection of children, constitute serious crimes. They are under the power of darkness, decadence, and corruption. And these things pass without any punishment from the course, because of the corruption of those who ought to perform justice.

When the violation is discovered by the enforcing authorities, it doesn't lead to criminal proceedings, where the result of which can be custodial sentences as well as fines. This is what happens when human beings relate to each other as objects to be consumed, and when the body becomes more and more a commodity.

The episode of Bibbiano scandal was carefully silenced and even the political refusal to ally with the Democratic Party, the dominant power in the area concerned and close to the judiciary. Although some of them were banned from practising the profession, and despite the temporary house arrest that the judge considered as a discipline, that cannot eradicate heinous crimes and their consequences. What is the value of authority if the responsible is Juan, elusive and sly?! The commitment of judge required them not to violate human rights for any reason. The penalties for these criminals must not be lifted. There is no room for impunity. Justice ought to be done for the victims, and criminals must receive a penalty equal to the value of the horrible crimes they committed.

Punishment should be as gross as the crime–execution is what this criminal gang deserves because their deception has no limits, and their crimes have no limits. They destroyed thousands of families; many people have died because of them, and many innocent people have committed suicide because of them, as well as that, many children have lived orphans because of them, and addicted to drugs because of them.

They and their associates are still engrossed in predation without fear. They are still unleashing the fulfillment of their personal desires without any punishment. For them, kidnapping children is an open-ended mine that should be drained safely, because of the existence of the impunity guarantee. There is no public interest or national interest. The power has turned into a constant abuse and permanent practice of exploitation of influence.

Those who are involved in the forgery, falsification and abuse are in breach of the Act and must face the trial. Unfortunately, this has never happened. In one of the hearings, the former manager of social services, Federica Anghinolfi, asked to return to her previous job without any shyness or embarrassment. This indicates the leniency of the judges on the one hand and underestimating the dangerous criminal practices they do on the other hand.

These heinous acts are aggressive against individuals and society. Impunity has become a worsening epidemic because of the spread of the culture of exemption and forgiveness for colleagues and friends. This may exacerbate the vulnerability of families to inhuman abuse as well as the assault and rape of their children.

On another side, children are not protected when they endure the worst possible abuse in foster families and in foster institutions. Even worse than this, several children have been adopted to sex shops, families who suffer from serious mental health conditions, and drug-addicted people.

Judges are responsible for hearing court cases and serving the best interests of the victims and communities. Judges are held to high legal and ethical standards, and they must treat all people in their courtrooms with fairness and impartiality. Judges, who show favouritism in courts or commit judicial errors which create unfair results, must face consequences.

Judges must avoid even the appearance of favouritism, so that the courts remain respected and reliable forums for justice. How can we get rid of tyranny if we do not prosecute these criminal officials?

Through our knowledge of the judge's duty, role, and responsibility towards the citizens without prosecuting the actions, tyranny will return to a new look and a new form and will take with it what is left of the innocents.

Italians and foreigners are declaring human rights violations, as well as their civil rights, are being stripped and taken from them and their families as a result of these atrocities. Being not responsive to the public, the government violates the law. Local government must be responsive to the People. This silence is the deepest violence. This silence is unacceptable!

The government must seek a remedy to injustices of a child protection system due to the manner in which parents are screened and assessed, and how incidents are resolved. Family Preservation Act should be practised. The government also must oversight Child Welfare; monitor the treatment of families by Child Protective Services, and the legislation, which makes termination of parental rights more difficult.

Parents should be allowed to petition for family reunification when their difficulties are overcome.

Juvenile courts and social services must be controlled. Judges have tremendous power to decide the fate of people and the future of their children. It is precisely for this reason that they must take great responsibility as much important as this task. They are not allowed to accept social workers' excuses, leniency, negligence, or grant them any empty mandate.

If it is revealed that there is collusion between a judge and social services that expresses a sense of common interests, the competent authorities must intervene as a matter of urgency. And the minister must step in to promote an external assessment of the environment in order to break the complicity and to restore balance. Many judges have destroyed entire families' lives and have not taken any consequences for their mistakes.

Imagine a society in which child kidnapping thrived, and without any deterrent methods and controls, the life of such a society would be hell where no one would be safe for their children and themselves. Accordingly, such a society would lose social safety and stability, and everyone would be going to use the protective methods that could protect them and their families. So, no one would turn to these institutions even if they would be still having problems where children could be seriously affected.

Absolutely, these problems could have been avoided if these institutions were safe and truly serving citizens. But they are turned into criminal organizations that intend to make illegal fortune in the shortest way. They steal children and they steal public money as well. All citizens should fight against this fraud and deception.

Punishment of the innocents

Flagrant violations of the Italian criminal courts that unjustly brand thousands of loving parents as criminals, as it has happened in my case which offers an especially eye-opening view of a criminal justice system that today imprison many innocent parents. They have been labeled enemies just because they fight against illegal kidnapping and adoption system.

Many criminal court judges have carried strangers' shame and hurt to their community. Unjustly accused parents are mishandled and manipulated by corrupt judges to ensure that charges against them are inevitable and due process is not carried out. The Italian Constitution is not on the agenda of these government institutions. As a result, citizens and foreigners are abused by these powers.

Many parents have been sentenced to several years of imprisonment without any crime committed by them. Even worse, children are brought to testify against their parents falsely after they have been brainwashed into believing that they have been abused by them. These unlimited demonic evil and incredible violations of international human rights interpret the inequality and injustice in Italian courts. Judges process cases in mere minutes, and nearly everyone pleads guilty.

The blind sentence starts punishing people long before they are convicted; it punishes the innocent, and it punishes conduct that never should have been a crime. Things are made worse when the court doesn't hold explicitly that the defendant has significant evidence of innocence. As a result, vast numbers of these people are good parents who love their children and never abused them— are stigmatized as criminals, impoverished through fines and fees, stripped of jobs, and deprived of their children forever.

When falsely accused parents complain about these lies, their complaints are ignored and are never considered. So it is difficult to prove these lies of social workers and psychologists. Corrupt theatrical judges sentence parents using the lowest standards of judicial evidence. A diligent, prudent, or reasonable investigation from criminal courts is sorely absent– that the masses do not know this and trust the system that needs to be understood. Family judicial processes are fraught with deception for the falsely accused.

Several parents have been imprisoned for assaulting their children, based on false reports that have been later found to be unfounded. My suffering from unfair judgment too has been continuing for many years. The potential for wrongful imprisonment cases have proven the unreliability of the criminal justice system. Due to many facts such as: Faulty psychiatry, falsification of documents, false accusation, manipulating the words of the children in order to admit that they have been abused, harsh interrogation techniques practices.

In addition to physical and mental abuses, the children are brainwashed and questioned by psychologists, psychiatrists, social workers, and educators, in many and many occasions. These false confessions coerced by these practices of torture have resulted in several convictions of many innocents.

In fact, judges don't investigate in the cases just because they belong to social services who feed these judges. All due process, constitutional rights and human rights are violated and manipulated by bad court judges.

Matters are judged and decided by accountable, unchallengeable in the court, and enforced by equally unaccountable and unchallengeable social services. The result is utter chicanery and corruption. The Judicial decisions violate the public trust.

For some strange reason, in most cases parents who abuse their children are ignored by the court and manage to escape punishment. It is for the benefit of the Juvenile Judges to use bad parents' acts as a justification to snatch children. This has been proven in many cases and has been illustrated by many lawyers; one of them described one of his practical experiences by saying:

''The mother presented to the court and gradually collected evidence or indications of the father's sexual abuse of the girl, and the court at first turned a deaf ear; then, faced with the new evidence presented by her mother, some judge told her to stop collecting them and

not to make complaints, because if she continued, the court would consider placing the child in a foster institute or with the father himself. Incredible, but true"

Conversely, many criminal judges make sentences based on false reports and false evaluation by social workers and psychiatrists, as it happened in my case. They fail to provide justice and fail to serve public order.

With no looking at the evidence, no investigating, and no distinguishing between truth and falsehood, judges lead to the displacement of children, the future of the nation. They lead to the dispersal of families and the killing of innocents.

Those judges who kidnapped my little girls and accused me unjustly could have led me to suicide like so many victims, but for my daughters I withstood. O judges, you make me lose the sense of my worth and of my dignity because of this oppression and humiliation.

You make me feel that my being is lost, and my motherhood is crushed. I became a hostage all the time to a permanent prison inside me. You disappointed me and my family and you killed all hopes inside us. Your stabbing at my children and your unexpected judgment are a great calamity.

"The accused is not considered guilty until the final sentence." This is how the Italian Constitution expresses itself in **article 27,** stating an apparently guaranteeing principle against the accused. Yet, in that "he is not considered guilty"; there is something that he does not convince. If a defendant is not found guilty, at least until the final sentence, what is considered then? Why define a legal status in negative instead of clearly stating that the accused is to be considered innocent until the final sentence of conviction?

It is as if the formula adopted by the Constituent Assembly leaves a margin of uncertainty and misunderstanding, confining the accused to a limbo, which is not even short-lived if we consider the duration of the trials. Therefore, the accused is imprisoned from the initial verdict before his innocence is ascertained, and no matter how long the final verdict arrives, he remains imprisoned for the entire period even if he is innocent.

There is a right to be considered innocent until proven otherwise. Since the lexicon has its importance. The accused is innocent until the contrary is legally proven, full stop. It should be a principle of elementary legal civilization, but it is not. It is not yet in Italy. In addition to that, procedures must be expedited for the citizens who are victims because even when a parent's innocence is recognized, error handling times are very long.

CHAPTER TWELVE

THE NEGLIGENT ROLE OF THE GOVERNMENT

Although children's rights are enshrined in the Italian constitution and international institutions, they are systematically violated. And although there are dual-parental laws and regulations that allow children to live in harmony with both parents, they are deprived of their rights; only to keep being beaten and bruised by the tyranny of these courts, funded by the local government.

Juvenile Judges, social workers, educators, psychologists, and psychiatrists who betray parents under the pretext of child protection, steal their children and drive them away from their natural, harmonious environment and their families. On paper since the 1970s foster institutions, cooperatives, and foundations have been hell on earth for children who were handed over to this facility for decades and systematically raped without government oversight.

The child protection crime rate has marked the increase in the country, from that time on a small and influential reformers group has been deciding that the time has come to point out the menace. They are doing it well and along, but they have faced the fear and malice at the part of "super-predators". Astonishingly this is so-called organized criminal organization are not people far from the law, but they are responsible for child protection as juvenile judges and social workers. And the government doesn't intend to make strict decisions. Thus continue the tyrant of child kidnapping and trafficking laws, which demonstrates the inadequacy of the juvenile justice system. To say those decisions are overbearing would be sensible.

It is an experimental abuse laboratory protected by the political class, a particular jurisdiction, with the tacit complicity of doctors and social workers, cancer of the power system. Known, recent and growing discoveries have revealed the reality of the judiciary which, from myth and mystery, is simply the same as the other powers, political, bureaucratic and administrative, and is an organic part of its system.

The government is a big supporter of the foster care industry

The Italian government has cultivated, nurtured, and protected adoption markets for many decades. The legal systems are corrupted by further government activities against the family. The government has become a huge supporter of the foster care and adoption industry; a system in which orphans are created for government funds. This system is a grinding machine on society. The trail of misery that leaves behind should not be tolerated by any decent human being, or by any decent society.

The Italian judiciary is aware of these situations in which children suffer and deceives them to exploit them more and better. The history of the Italian government has yet to do justice to the stolen childhood; rights are forgotten, misled, lost, and swept under the rug like dust. The deaf, dumb, blind judicial system adopts crazy psychiatry based on violence, bullying, harassment, abuse and rape. In short, it is endless suffering.

In this way, children become essential and indispensable objects to feed and ensure a corrupt business. The state funds foster care and adoption. But foster care and adoption are BIG BUSINESS and BIG DISTRUCTION to community members. They obtain billions of euros each year illegally, and their "goods" are children who in many cases should have been left in their homes. This money is shared by judges, psychiatrists, social workers and everyone who participate in destroying families

Everyone is chasing this public money, but public money should not be spent making our children a commodity. There are thousands of children who have been ripped from their homes all because of money. Children are not tools, objects, or things, but rights holders. In any society, they represent innocence and the future. This self-enclosed predation betrays a strange kind of blindness. The current system in which public money is tied to foster care and adoption makes our children a commodity to sell. If public funds are spent, the terminology must be clear and precise.

It is in the hands of business committees operating in illegitimacy, which manage competitions for magistrates, the careers of magistrates, the assignment of important posts, the persecution of magistrates who do not bow to the system, the protection of those who serve it, the facilitation of the market of court sentences because, in a world where everything is becoming a commodity, even people, sentences are also commodities. The pockets of tyranny are going unchecked without recourse.

From the "Angel and Demon" scandal and from previous dossiers, the chapter of justice that deals with minors was opened in juvenile courts. It is known that there is currently a turnover of around 5 billion per year for the placement of minors in private institutions that make profits with their partners or collaborators, such as Juvenile Judges, magistrates, and professionals who entrust children to these private institutions, and whose fees sometimes exceed 400 euros per day. Statistics show that there are now approximately 500,000 children who have been removed from their parents.

Forced expulsion and interventions that are carried out against the will of parents harshly the law that was implemented without taking into consideration the personal pain of children is a device that was limited to satisfying material needs ignoring the most profound needs.

With false accusations, great crimes committed

With false accusations and hidden justifications such as parental incompetence and inappropriateness, big human crimes are committed to destroy the family, the backbone of society. The local government is not responsive to the people despite these violations. Social workers are not held accountable, and it is not a felony when they misrepresent the evidence. They have no oversight, accountability, and consequences. Failure to take this into account makes everyone co-responsible for the mass degradation of human civilization.

Violence against children is the emblem of a deteriorating civil coexistence, a dying civilization that has lost the values necessary for its survival. Childhood is stolen from many children. We parents were never allowed to have contact them again. They are threatened and forced to declare falsehood to the detriment of the parent. This is the process after "legal abduction" in order to sell it in an adoption scheme.

Children's social services and juvenile courts steal our children and public money. Children are snatched from their loving families without probable cause, and where there is no imminent danger. Our children are placed in foster care with paedophiles, rapists, drug users, those who have records of assaults, and are then placed for adoption to strangers, avoiding family members for possible placement.

Child Protective Services also target new mothers who are hospitalized to deliver their babies. They snatch these newborns directly from their mother's breast with the help of the doctors. Doctors and nurses detain young mothers in the hospital until the child social workers come and remove their babies from them where there is no abuse, drug addictions, neglect, etc...

Child protection system enables social workers to legally take a baby by force from its mother at birth. Often on the grounds that the child MAY suffer emotional abuse sometime in the future. Judges, social workers, doctors, nurses, psychologists, teachers, pharmaceutical companies correlate together to rip children away from their Bio-families by any means necessary, in order to obtain this Federal Money.

Parents and extended family members are not given due process, constitutional, civil, disability, or basic human rights in this corrupt system. They are not given adequate council, reasonable opportunity for reunification. They are also systematically being denied their civil, constitutional, and human rights on the "hearsay" and fraudulent testimony of public officers nationwide.

Neither judges nor officers of the court observe parent's Civil/Constitutional Rights. These rights are blatantly ignored and denied by both officers of the court, as well as local and state government employees bound to uphold the Constitution of Italy.

Child welfare issues and human rights abuses are impacting children and families nationally. Families are being abused by social workers and juvenile Courts throughout Italy. Families' civil rights are violated through family court proceedings as well as all due process and constitutional rights are violated and manipulated by family court judges, District Attorneys, Commissioners of social services departments, and social workers.

Thousands of families have evidence and proof that they have been wronged by these institutions and have reported these issues. Many of these complaints have been dismissed. The additional drama of these children is that they're not being heard whereas their voice should have a fundamental role in decisions that affect them, according to the law.

Their voices remain inaudible and that is the direction of the institutions in which they are welcomed, where psychological fulfillment is the least of their goals for the child. These children quickly get tired of complaining because they consider adults completely incapable of understanding and acting in their favour. They feel crushed in a suffocating grip, and they cannot wait to come out of adulthood. But even this is a difficult option to take up with their experience of abandonment, cruelty, and loss of meaning that is accompanying their broken souls and their submission to new dangers and new manipulations.

There has been surprisingly little research on the long-term effects of foster care, but the research that has been done concludes that children who go through the foster system suffer tremendous emotional damage and are three times more likely to experience bad outcomes.

Many of them are given to unsuitable foster families and to awful child foster institutions, and a "bad house" is often better than "bad outcomes" that include teenage pregnancy, not competing high school, incarceration, substance abuse, and homelessness. They are five times more likely to commit suicide and eight times more likely to have serious psychiatric disorders.

Adoption leaves the child with more trauma, and even sadder. Many children are told that they were removed from abusive parents and adopted to be protected. However, a lot of former adopted children are miserable and runaways from huge problems, while they feel that they have no future, no families, and no relatives.

They are tired of being angry, ashamed, alone, and choose to walk a new path, sharing their experience, strength, and hope while building a bridge to new life and healing. Unfortunately, this is a difficult dream to come true without a solid professional preparation, without economic autonomy, and above all with the fragile personality of those who are bitterly disappointed and frustrated.

Kidnapping minors, erasing their identities, and trading them become a process that humiliates and crushes thousands of children across Italy. The identity and narrative that are imposed on them are defeatist and leading to self-loathing. Identity is an intrinsic idea of one's life and the struggle of it often happens, but this process can be more difficult for adoptees.

Many individuals experience a sense of alienation and a sense of loss towards their biological parents which can create considerable confusion and an adoption identity crisis, which can sometimes contribute to feelings of anxiety, depression or low self-esteem.

The purpose of the foster care system is to provide a safe haven for children, helping them to cross the bridge from foster care to ageing out, but sadly the bridge leads to nowhere. Welfare reform has thrown more children into poverty and increased their chances of placement into foster care. This harsh treatment of juvenile offenders translates into the increased incarceration of children.

All of this completely destroys families. Child protection authorities are taking custody of children at alarming rates, and in doing so they are dismantling social networks that are critical to community welfare. The lives, health, and well-being of our children are in clear and present danger as long as the department of child and family services has the power to remove them from our care without cause, without warrants or justification.

As public service employees in all sectors of government continue to fail to uphold the law or protect those they were selected to serve and protect under the Constitution of Italy. The Italian judiciary is aware of these situations in which children suffer, deluding it to exploit it more and better. The most remarkable cases often rise to the level of news and occupy the front pages of newspapers for a few days until the scandal subsides and the situation returns to the concealment of its identity.

It is time that the state must fix the corruption within the system. Justice and truth must emerge. Citizens' initiatives must intensify without associative, political or confessional flags. To move them is the civic conscience, the desire for solidarity with the families and children affected by the abuse. The silence and the complicity of those who have governed the country are very serious.

Shameful is the silence of those who profess to be leftists as "Champions of Social Justice." A country that cannot protect children is an uncivilised, a disabled and backward country. Because of the deep silence from the government, a huge number of children die many times but are still alive.

The concern for raising the level of childcare, family matters, needs, and issues as the family is the cell of society. And childhood is the focus of social development in its comprehensive concept. Not only because children are men and women of the future, and the basis for the renaissance and progress of nations. Not so because they are the most vulnerable and in need of care. The interest in children goes back mainly to being (human); they have basic rights that must be guaranteed by the state, no matter how rich or poor it is.

The process of paying attention to the situation of children and their rights cannot be separated from the process of paying attention to human rights issues.

The story of childhood in Italy is a story that talks about the failure of the government, the lack of courage, and the passive neglect of children.

It is necessary to reform a system that no longer works; Child Protective Services have become dominated by so many wrong-headed people, and the public money comes to fund them. Are they deluded that they think they are doing well or is there a New World political agenda driving them? Why do prosecutors go along with them? Why do police departments make arrests based on little or no evidence? Why do the corrupt adoption reverberations continue despite the scandals?

Corruption is the Child Protective Services' greatest problem. Not parents' poverty. Not parents' abuse. Not parents' incompetence. Social workers, under the assumption that they are doing the ''public good'' protecting children and assisting families, can forcefully remove children without giving cause or reason.,

A holistic approach is needed to fight the systematic corruption that has been abounding in Child Protective Services over many years. The government's immediate response and proposed actions are too modest.

In-depth reforms are needed to secure the corruption-free future that people are demanding. The solution should be participatory, and the government should engage with civil society and citizens in order to make lasting change and rebuild trust within a new Child Protection System.

The scale of illegal foster care and adoption challenge requires wholesale, systemic reform that leaves no space for the old patterns and players to retain control over a corrupt business. The rigorous anti-corruption reforms needed have not been made. The protests we're seeing across Italy all result from governments failing to meet the demands that their citizens have been making.

The government must act now to stop these gruesome practices once and for all. STOP the federal funding to Child Protective Services - to kidnap our children! STOP supporting this clear Misappropriation of Funding and Abuse of Authority by Officers of Government institutions, it is happening on Italy soil and being orchestrated by own government, specifically child social services, juvenile courts, and family courts in every city across Italy.

CHAPTER THIRTEEN

THE CORRUPT SYSTEM DOESN'T LAST FOREVER

To those who fight us for our blood and flesh.
To those who fight us for our children, the core of our hearts. To those who trample upon the dignity of our beloved ones and the dignity of our motherhood.

Who are you and what is the power on earth that allows you to destroy the lives of citizens and immigrants?!
Is there no force or human rights court that can stop you? Where have you got this power that you use to demolish the humanity?! Where have you got these dead hearts that throw children and parents under your desires? Where have you got these consciences that swore not to betray, and for betrayal are the racers?

Your cruelty led to the suicide of many, the imprisonment of thousands, and the death of others of heartbreak. This is an asset for you as you believe. Because you want to get rid of those who stand in your way. How can the happiness of your hearts be at the expense of the sadness of others?
How would you like your children to be happy at the expense of the deep sorrow of other children, whose hearts are as pure as your children's?

How can you build the future of your children at the expense of crushing innocent people? The happiness that you are looking for in this way is a fake happiness, build on unjust, exploitive gains on children's flesh and parents' floods of tears: "As you condemn, you will be condemned, and tomorrow you will receive the rewards." Because when you sleep, the eyes of the oppressed can't sleep. They raise their complaints and prayers to heaven. They are certain that if the justice of the earth fails, the justice of heaven will not fail, even if this justice is delayed but it will come true.

Do not tell me that it is the earth's laws which always govern, as I heard from you. Do not tell me that you are the strongest because the power is in your hands, as the Juvenile Judge, Salvatore, once told me: "We are stronger than you ma'am, you must be stronger than us to get your daughters back." It sounds incredible but it's true!

The Lord of the world is stronger than you and all creatures. He is certainly with the oppressed and the patient, and he promises them victory. Even if it seems to you that the demons won at first, but they will be defeated definitively because 'Satan's plots are always weak'.

Your evil deeds will follow you for the rest of your lives, your children and your offspring. You will live bitterness and grief, and you will cry a lot as you have caused so many to cry because someone who sows evil will reap nothing but thorns. Many despots have overwhelmed throughout history, but all have been doomed to failure.

No corrupt system can last forever. These atrocities will be exposed and everyone who has participated in the system will be called to give an account, because what is false will not last forever. The defeat of truth is temporary, and its victory is always eternal. Those who deceive us think that they should savour the pleasure of victory gained through falsehood while it lasts. Who has seen the future? Who will see anything anyway?

"We will forget it and so will everyone else," they tell themselves, mockingly. However, that is a judgment based on falsehood. The future is the shadow of the present. The future cannot be created without the present.

A person under the influence of falsehood can rejoice in the momentary jubilation of having acquired wealth, fame, or honour, but such a soul cannot experience peace of mind or the serene satisfaction that comes with untainted achievements.

Your hearts are filled with greed. You have hearts of stone, or even worse in hardness; there are stones out of which rivers gush forth, but your hearts out of which evils gush forth. There is no truth in your mouths, nor a word you speak can be trusted; your tongues practice lies and deceit. Your hands write nothing but forgery. Most parents don't find out your reality until it's too late.

Is your real job serving citizens or quick profit and owning real estate on the skins of the weak? Isn't this a slander in the citizen's service institutions? Isn't this a disgrace in Italian courts? Because of your malice, mountains can be removed, and hearts can be shattered. Your malice makes the beloved an enemy, the wise a crazy, and the dear servile. Your malice has led to the fact that children, when they grow up, begin to take drugs and suffer from severe psychological diseases that cannot be cured.

Oh Judges, you are participating in all of this in violation of local and international law. You are not providing justice and you are not serving public order. Without strong and effective examination of evidence, and without distinguishing truth from falsehood, you are contributing to the displacement of children, the future of the nation.

You are participating in the deterioration of the nation, and you are participating in the separation of families and the killing of innocent people. Do you know that many of those who are unjustly imprisoned are more honourable than those who accused them, and those who imprisoned them? Oh oppressors, does it not ache for your hearts to awaken from the darkness of oppression?

Oh unjust judges, how many rights have you deprived, and how many children have you tortured, and how many

mothers and fathers have you grieved?
How can your hearts rejoice at the expense of others' wounding hearts?
The worst kind of injustice is done in the name of unjust laws. How families can give their confidence again in these beasts that eat the children of the world, destroying citizens and immigrants.

I still find it hard to believe that something like this happened to me. For 16 years I have been allowed no phone calls, no visits, no letters, absolutely nothing. It is 16 years of lost smiles, lost hugs and lost time spent together as a family. I was not even being told where they were, so every night I went to sleep not knowing where they were, the abduction of my children is the most traumatic experience of my life.

This is how The Child Protection Services left me to live without a dream, without desires, but with shock, disbelief, frustration and despair. Despite this I live on the remnants of hoping to get my daughters back.

Scatter me oh waiting! Scatter me oh pain!
But I am certain that my daughters will come back to me. Hundreds of dewdrops to greet the dawn, hundreds of bees in purple clover lilies, and hundreds of butterflies in the garden, but there is only ONE MOTHER for every human being all over the world, and they CAN'T be two!

You want to kill love and motherhood, but motherhood is the heart of freedom, and there is no power on earth that can seize it. Motherhood is the sun that illuminates human life, and who can prevent the sun from rising!

We will defeat you, criminals!
You are not able to extinguish the light of life in us.
We will defeat you with the tenderness of mothers.
We will defeat you with the clemency of fathers.
We will defeat you with the innocence of our children.
We will not forget your evils.

You, who have stolen the joy from the eyes of our children, we will not forgive you.

We are the love and peace, and you are the hatred and malice!
We are the warmth and safety, and you are the fear and cold!
We are the hope and light, and you are the despair and darkness!
We are the joy and happiness, and you are the worry and grief!

Children deserve better, and families deserve better.
We, The People, we have a burning desire for justice.
We are coming together to stand against these tyrannical regime.

We hope that you will read this, address these issues, and help us to get justice for every family and every child, wrongfully victimized by the corrupt system. If you do not, then you too are part of the problem and just as guilty and will be held accountable by The People and the Human Rights Tribunal.

We Do Not Forget! We Will Not Forgive!

ABOUT THE AUTHOR

Mina Ghiate, originally from Morocco, is the author of her true account of a sixteen-year ordeal with the Italian justice system that stole her two daughters and accused her unfairly.

Mina has obtained a University Degree in English Literature in 1996, University of Arts and Human Sciences in Casablanca.

Her first book *The Legal Mafia* is a voice for those who want to defend human rights in good faith, and those who want to stop crimes against humanity.